CELEBRATE!
Your Festival Handbook
CHRISTMAS

hachette
INDIA

First published in India 2011 by Hachette India
(Registered name: Hachette Book Publishing India Pvt Ltd)
An Hachette UK company
www.hachetteindia.com

SRD

ISBN 978-93-5009-342-9

Hachette Book Publishing India Pvt Ltd
4th & 5th Floors, Corporate Centre;
Plot No. 94, Sector 44; Gurgaon 122003, India

Typeset in Goudy Old Style 11.6/14.8 and Futura 10.5/15
by Eleven Arts, New Delhi

Printed and bound in India by
Manipal Technologies Limited, Manipal

FSC
www.fsc.org
MIX
Paper from
responsible sources
FSC™ C043100

Contents

Super Christmas Stories

The Comet Chaser

Anu Kumar

'Can't we be home for Christmas?' Alia must have asked her mother this for the hundredth time. Despite the fact that she didn't know much about Christmas, especially not the way it was celebrated back on Earth.

'Home?' her mother looked at her reproachfully.

'I meant Earth, of course,' Alia said. Mom must have explained things to her ninety-nine times already. One more time wouldn't change things much.

On the planet they were on, there were no days and nights. There was just an unending twilight. That was why the planet was called Purple Lighting, for the sky was always a shade of purple that never changed, and Alia knew it was likely to be so till the time they were here. And that, according to Mom's science director in the central space headquarters on Earth, meant at least six more Earth months. Inside their space station, days and nights were artificially simulated, and that was how they kept track of days, weeks and months and occasions like Christmas, too.

Mom was a space geologist and she was here to study rock samples on this planet. She held meetings via satellite with other scientists all across the Thousandth Galaxy. And she went out on long explorations outside the space station, digging inside mountains, searching among the many craters that dotted the planet for minerals and rocks that looked of interest. Outside the space station, temperatures were always below freezing, and sometimes sandstorms would blow across from the nearest planet called Arid Yellow, where Alia's best friend Raul stayed with his parents.

Twice an Earth week, they could see the spaceship Zircon fly across the southern skies. Sometimes it stopped by their planet, dropping food supplies, the colours Mom needed for her paintings and sundry other things that were required. Mom painted whenever she had some free time. She said it was her way to add some other colours to the purple world around her.

Mom took care of most things at home. Alia, for her part, joined up for school via satellite. She played tennis with a robot, and sometimes she took the spacecab to the nearby planet where Raul stayed so they could study together.

Raul knew as little as Alia did about Christmas. Moreover, unlike Alia, he had rarely been back on Earth.

It was their Earth teacher who had explained to them what Christmas was. And so while they knew about Christmas, and could talk about it, they had never experienced it. And the more Alia learnt about it, she knew it was something to be experienced.

And all this made her ask Mom the same question, in different ways.

'It can't be Christmas if we stay here. It never snows here, and the trees are not green. And there is no chance of a Santa Claus turning up here either.'

Mom made a carefully considered reply. 'You shouldn't believe in Santa Claus,' she said, for she was ever the practical scientist. 'And they should update stuff like that on the syllabus, don't you think? Maybe someone should write of different Christmases?'

'Well, I can't imagine Santa Claus as a robot,' said Alia, 'carrying bags of gifts on a motorized sleigh with cruise-control.' And then she went on, 'Christmas is about the exchange of presents, too. Christmas is a lovely time for giving things to one another. And no, Mom, I really am not being greedy.'

'No,' said Mom smiling, in the unexpected way she had. It drove grooves into her cheeks and crinkled up her cheeks and Alia felt all was right with the world again. 'You are not greedy ever. You wouldn't have come away with me here, otherwise, for so long. But you know, giving can happen in other ways, too. Even if you just think of someone and wish something nice for the person.'

That was a profound thought, and Alia knew she would have to think over it later. Some of Mom's serious thoughts were made for mulling over. They were 'deep' in that sense.

So she changed the subject. 'Yes, it would be nice to have different Santa Clauses. For example, even if he does decide to come so far away, he couldn't possibly come in sleigh pulled by reindeer. Do you think he could breathe in the thin air and would his reindeer have enough to eat?'

She must have looked woebegone because Mom hugged her and made her a promise: Next year she would enjoy a real Earth Christmas

This, of course, made Alia ask the question she shouldn't have.

'Will Daddy be there?'

It made Mom's face cloud over. The twinkle vanished from her eyes and her lips formed a thin, straight line. Alia could have kicked herself. It was all their different careers. Dad lived right at the other end of the universe. Sometimes she received mails from him that really took ages because he was many, many light years away. He was so far that he could never project himself onto the magnetic screen, which allowed you to see people even a hundred light years away. In his lightning mails to Alia he had told her he studied comets. And as comets travelled very far and in strangely elliptical orbits, Dad spent all his time following them. Rare were the occasions when Alia and her mother had actually met him.

She counted. Yes, Dad had wished her on every birthday, but she had last seen him when she was five.

'Let's see . . . he could be busy,' was all Mom said for now.

The week before Christmas, Mom sprang a surprise. She had arranged for Alia to have a good Christmas. She had hired a special spacecab, for on Christmas day all across the universe, you had to book in advance. And it was arranged that Alia and Raul would spend the day at a Christmas theme park not too far away. It had a snow park, robot reindeers and even a walking-talking Santa Claus.

'What about you, Mom?' Alia asked.

'Don't worry about me. I've seen enough Christmases in my life. I have a special conference and this is the only time all the scientists across the galaxy are available. Besides, this is my special Christmas present to you—have a great time.'

Alia nodded, too overwhelmed to speak. She remembered what her mother had said. Sometimes Christmas is more than giving presents; you could wish something wonderful for someone. And secretly, Alia wished for a wonderful Christmas for her mom too. She hoped perhaps a spectacular star shower would happen, that the sky would turn into one vast colour palette that the dome of dull purple that covered them would transform into a high ceiling containing every rainbow colour.

Mom was happiest when she painted. She always said there wasn't much colour in this part of the universe.

It appeared much more colourful through the giant telescope from where you could see quasars and faraway spinning galaxies, spiralling comets, and it was the Earth that looked the most beautiful of all. Blue and white with those wisps of cloud like feathery necklaces all around it. It always made Alia catch her breath. 'Soon, soon, at least for next Christmas, we will be there,' she now whispered.

She told Mom not to be up when the special space bus came early that Christmas morning. 'You will barely have time to rest, with the conference continuing over two days, so don't worry about me,' she assured her.

That Christmas Eve night, Alia was too excited to even sleep, but she must have. For it was the noise that woke her, a totally different, hard-to-place sound that she had never heard before. It began with a low buzzing; there was the slow tolling of bells and then she heard the sound of something metallic falling. Last, there was the sound of the rocky pebbles rising and falling against the glass walls of the space station.

It couldn't be the spacecab. It came with a low musical horn all its own. She hoped the noise hadn't woken her Mom up, and so draping a cloak over herself for the thin atmosphere outside could freeze you in an instant, Alia cautiously made her way outside. In the purple light, she saw the rock pebbles still flying around, and next to a funnily designed vehicle, a spider with wings like a grasshopper's, she saw someone else, too.

It was a man weighed down by the heavy dark cloak he was wearing, on his head a helmet with antennae protruding from it in every direction. He was struggling with the oxygen tank on his back. The tubes leading from it were entangled in his cloak pockets and he was trying hopelessly to sort it all out.

The oxygen tank which was a fairly old model told Alia that he came from a pretty distant place that was very behind the times. For here, you simply recharged a cell on your breathing pad strapped to your back, and this produced enough oxygen to last one Earth day.

Alia rushed to help him, and he stood without moving as she sorted out the wires. His pockets contained small machines of every kind—calculators, decoding devices, special lights and scoop-up machines, and it took her quite a while to unwind the trapped oxygen tube. She tried to begin a conversation with him but he was as silent as he was still. She had a subject called 'space etiquette' in which she had been taught that some space beings could be reserved, while they took in their new surroundings. Sometimes their sensory organs were slower to respond. Perhaps that was why this particular space being refused to take off his helmet and his special anti-radiation glasses as well. Alia wondered why he didn't for he must be uncomfortable. Then he coughed and it splattered the glass face of his helmet and he blew it away by pressing a smoke valve.

Alia smiled, hoping the cough was his way of saying thank you. Other beings had other ways of expressing themselves, the etiquette teacher had instructed, and it was important never to reach a conclusion too quickly.

But when the stranger spoke at last, it was in low measured tones and Alia knew he had to be an Earthman. 'What is this place?' he asked.

'It's called Purple Lighting, till a proper name is worked out,' she answered.

And this time the Earthman broke out into a prolonged bout of coughing. It took him quite a bit to recover, and Alia stared at him in some anxiety. She wondered if she should suggest her mom's special temperature-raising shower that was supposed to be very effective for a space-travel-induced cough.

'Oh no, no,' said the stranger for he was after all a stranger, even if he were an Earthman. 'I am fine. I am on my way to a Christmas celebration.'

The pat manner of his response made Alia suspicious. When someone offers a too simple an answer, and too quickly, you can be sure something was wrong.

'Are you Santa Claus, by chance? Or some kind of Santa . . .'

He turned his glassy-helmeted face to her. 'No, I am not, I wish people wouldn't compare me to Santa. I try to look so different.'

He did seem affronted and Alia hastened to offer him an apology.

'It's all right,' said the Earthman, 'I *do* things differently, too. You know, I don't just bring gifts, but I hope and try to make people's wishes come true.'

'That must be difficult,' said Alia, remembering what her mother had said, about presents being of various kinds. 'I mean gifts can be so easy to get or buy, but wishes could be so . . .' She hunted for the right word.

'Elusive?' suggested the Earthman.

'What does elusive mean?' she asked in turn.

'Things that you think are far from your grip but which actually could be close enough. Or things that are within your reach, but you don't know how to find them . . . think about it.'

'I daresay you have a point.' He wasn't such a difficult being as she had thought. Maybe he was just a different kind of Santa Claus. All of them couldn't be red-cloaked, bearded and hearty.

But he was looking up at the sky, unmindful of the cosmic dust spattering on the glass as he said again, 'Or wishes could work in other ways. Sometimes you think you want one thing, but you get something else. And that some other wish might turn out to be a far better thing, after all.

'I see.'

'And wishes work best when you want them for others.'

'I see.'

In space etiquette, it was best to respond by showing the other being you are following his train of thought.

But the Earthman didn't seem to hear her, 'For example, I wouldn't have wished to have landed here. I know there's a very busy scientist in this place who perhaps wouldn't like my presence here at all.'

'That's not the case,' Alia came stoutly to the scientist's defence without thinking how he could have known about her mom. 'She's busy, and will be in conferences all these two days. She's giving up her Christmas for some very important work. Sometimes she has to adjust to communicating with scientists who could be in a different time space, and she could be exhausted.'

He laughed, 'Whoa there, you didn't let me finish. I was saying that I would never have wanted to land here but I got the most unexpected present. A Christmas present too.'

His voice sounded very wobbly, and the smoke had clouded over his visor again.

Alia stared at him, but she couldn't really ask him direct questions. That was one of the rules of space etiquette. You were not supposed to ask personal or direct questions. Questions were classified as embarrassing.

'Do you think if I wished to see my father, it would be granted?' she asked.

'It would be, or it could work other ways? You could wish for something else for someone else.'

'I want my mother to be happy,' she said simply. 'I don't know what could make her happy, but I do want to see her smile more often.'

She thought of her mother's smile as she said this. The smile that crinkled up her eyes, drove deep grooves into her cheeks, that lit up the world around her.

'My mom would be happy to see more colour here, or maybe she would want to hear from my dad. But they are too proud. And then they think I am too young to understand.'

'Hmm, why, you must be eleven by now.'

How does this Earthman know this, she started to wonder, but right then she heard the low musical laughter of the spacecab. It whistled a chirpy tune as it made its way through storm clouds and its powerful headlights cut through the purple twilight.

'Oh dear, the cab's here.'

'And it's Christmas morning . . . I suppose you are ready to go?' said the Earthman.

'What about you?' She asked, remembering his spacecraft was possibly damaged and he had to get it repaired somehow

'I am not sure. I'm actually monitoring something that makes an appearance every 200 Earth years. And the best position could be something from the planet that's forty light years away. It could take me a day's journey. I might take more time now.'

Alia thought it over. Christmas was a time for giving, for doing something for others too. Her mother had said this, and so had the Earthman.

'You could go in this cab, take my place in it. Mom will be happy if I spend Christmas with her. She arranged for this because I cribbed so much about being alone.'

'You are sure?'

Alia nodded, not finding the words to respond. Perhaps her teacher of space etiquette would understand.

'Thank you, thank you.'

And he leaned forward and kissed her through his helmet.

'I will write to you once I reach.'

'How will it get to me?'

'There's only one little girl with a wonderful way with words on the planet of Purple Lighting,' he said. And he snorted as he took in deep gulps of oxygen, bounced on his feet, and scattering the pebbles, he made his way towards the waiting spacecab.

Then, as if he had remembered something, he returned. Leaning down, he told her, speaking slowly as if he wanted her to remember every word. 'And watch out, you could see something colourful in the western skies before the day is over. Something colourful and sweeping. I can bet it's unlike anything you've seen before.'

It was only as the cab picked up speed, spreading out its white albatross-like wings, did it strike Alia as somewhat strange that the Earthman had known exactly how old she was. He had said she was eleven. She stared till the storm clouds had totally enveloped the cab and she couldn't hear its musical singing any more.

Mom and Alia had a quiet Christmas. Mom baked a cake, Alia played something on her violin and then in the afternoon, Mom started painting a special portrait of Alia.

It was much later when, looking out, Alia had already begun to wonder if the Earthman had meant what he had said, if something extraordinary would actually appear in the sky.

It happened just as the lights dimmed in the space station. There was a blinding flash of yellow, the radar picked up a swishing noise and small sparks and pebbles flew everywhere. As they looked through the glass windows, they saw, just as the Earthman had predicted, the western sky awash with a silver light. A golden blob appeared and behind it a silver band of light, with dancing flashes of red dots embedded in it. It was a brilliant star, and it had a very long tail.

It painted the sky in different colours as it streaked past—red, yellow, purple, and a lovely shade of aquamarine that was her mother's favourite shade.

'It's a comet,' said Alia holding her breath.

'So it is, so it is,' said Mom slowly, 'I wonder if your father knows about it.'

'Mom,' Alia turned to say, but her mother looked more radiant than she ever had before, and Alia smiled and didn't say anything more.

Mom pressed her nose against the glass window, and murmured softly, her arm around her daughter's shoulder. 'It's the loveliest Christmas I've ever had. You being here and this coloured-up beautiful world.'

Alia thought she wouldn't say anything today about the Earthman just then. Christmas was already special. All these other surprises could light up other days.

The Cupboard

Deepa Agarwal

The news Alpana had been waiting for arrived barely a week before Christmas.

Papa was the one who brought it. He surprised them by arriving earlier than he normally did that day, a few minutes before the clock struck seven. It was as dark as a coal mine outside and eleven-year-old Alpana and her mother were snuggled on the sofa in the living room, with the front door shut tight against the winter chill. It was colder than usual this year and some of the hills that surrounded the town already showed a sprinkling of white.

'Mamma, I think we should take out the Christmas tree ornaments tomorrow,' Alpana was saying when the sound of a familiar footstep on the veranda steps made her start up. 'Papa!' she exclaimed. 'Oh, I was hoping that you'd come early today!'

'And I guessed it.' Papa smiled and tapped her cheek with a chilly finger. 'How nice and cosy it is in here!' He put down his doctor's bag to warm his hands at the fire that was licking around the pine logs. 'When are you going to decorate the tree, my dear? Christmas is almost here.'

'Tomorrow, I thought,' Alpana replied. She chewed her lower lip. 'Only . . .'

'Only, you were wondering if Nandita was coming. And you wanted to wait for her?' Papa's eyes twinkled behind his glasses.

Alpana flung a quick glance at Mamma before she replied, 'Y-es . . .'

Mamma's large eyes were expressionless as Papa said, gazing into the fire. 'I got a call from her today. She'll be here tomorrow afternoon.'

'Tomorrow?' Alpana couldn't help jumping up in delight.

'That *is* good news, isn't it,' Mamma said evenly. 'We'll have a proper family get together this time. Imagine, I decided to air her room just today. It's been shut for such a long time. All we need to do now is to make up the bed and put fresh towels in the bathroom.'

'Wonderful!' Papa beamed. 'I'll bring the Christmas tree in tomorrow morning.'

'And when Nandita Didi arrives, we can decorate it together.' Alpana sighed happily.

The buttery December sunshine warmed Alpana's face as she snipped stems of bright red poinsettia flowers from the tall stand near the gate, trying not to get their sticky milk on her fingers. What a brilliant contrast they made to the vivid blue of the sky! Inside the house, they made everything look Christmassy immediately. She'd put some in the living room and the rest in Nandita Didi's bedroom.

As she entered the house, the rich aroma of *gajar ka halwa* cooking came to her. The cakes had been baked more than a week ago, but Mamma and her helpers would be busy preparing all kinds of goodies till Christmas day itself.

'Which vase shall I put in Nandita Didi's room?' she called out to her mother.

'You know.' Muffled by the distance, Mamma's voice sounded deeper than usual. 'The tall brass one. The poinsettias will look nice in that.'

It was her sister's favourite vase. Alpana knew that well. Why had she asked Mamma? Maybe she wanted some reassurance from her. Such an old, old vase. Alpana hadn't seen one like it in anyone else's house.

Entering the room, she got the usual fluttery feeling in her belly—kind of nervous and guilty. Was she venturing into a place she wasn't supposed to? She loved her older sister wholeheartedly, but sometimes she felt like an interloper in this room. As she placed the vase on the old fashioned dresser, she couldn't help sneaking a glance at the cupboard.

It was old too, practically antique, like most of the furniture in this room. And it was always locked. Only

Nandita had the key. Once when Alpana was much younger, beside herself with curiosity, she had asked her what there was inside the cupboard. 'My secret treasures,' Nandita had replied with a laugh that sounded tinny.

'Treasures! What treasures, Didi? Can't I see them? Please . . .' When Nandita did not reply, she had said with a pout, 'But I tell you everything, don't I?'

'That doesn't mean I have to,' Nandita had snapped. 'Learn to respect other people's privacy!'

Alpana had gasped, she was so shocked. Her sister had never spoken to her like that, so harshly. How could she? Granted, she was much older—a full fourteen years older. Granted too . . . that they were not real sisters . . . they had different mothers. Nandita's mother had died when she was eight years old, and five years later Papa had married Mamma. But weren't they even closer than real sisters? Alpana could never ever dream of having the slightest tiff with Nandita Didi or making her sad in any way.

She left Nandita's room in tears that day. But she blamed herself rather than her sister.

Why had she pestered her to open the cupboard? How could she have forgotten? Once, when she was looking for her, Alpana found that Nandita had bolted the door of her room shut. She knocked, called out to her to open it, but there was no reply.

Suddenly Mamma appeared and pulled her away. 'Don't ever do that again!' she'd said. 'You mustn't disturb Nandita

Didi when she wants to be alone in her room. She needs her privacy.'

'Privacy?' Alpana had wrinkled her brows. 'But everyone can come into my room whenever they wish!'

'That's different,' Mamma had said, giving her a hug. 'You're a little girl and Nandita's grown up.'

'That's not fair,' Alpana had protested. But somewhere, deep inside, she knew it was more than that.

Nandita Didi arrived just as they were about to have lunch. She ran into the house, her delicate face flushed with excitement.

'Alpu!' she cried, hugging her. She tried to pick Alpana up in her arms and whirl her around.

'Oh my God, you've really grown big,' she said, when she couldn't, gasping for breath. She turned to Mamma and gave her a polite peck on her cheek.

'You're seeing me after a year and a half, Didi,' Alpana pouted.

'Has it really been that long?' Nandita narrowed her eyes, then looked away.

'It is. Last winter you went on a trip with your friends so you didn't come for Christmas . . . and in the summer you said you couldn't get leave,' Alpana rattled off.

Nandita was silent for a few minutes. Then she said in an extra bright voice, 'Hmm . . . I'll make up for it this time . . . Why is the Christmas tree standing there all bare?'

'I was waiting for you to come, Didi,' Alpana said softly.

'All right, we'll get cracking after lunch!' Nandita clasped her hands.

'Er . . . wouldn't you like to rest for a while?' Mamma asked. 'It's a long journey, coming here from the city.'

'I'm not tired at all,' Nandita proclaimed in the slightly brusque tone of voice she used with Mamma.

Alpana's throat choked up. Why didn't her sister feel as happy to see Mamma as she was to see Alpana? But . . . how could anyone like the person who had replaced their own mother?

The Christmas tree was a-glitter with coloured glass balls, silvery bells, tinsel and bright with all the different ornaments they had collected over the years when Papa got home that evening, even earlier than yesterday.

'*Now* it feels that Christmas is just around the corner!' His smile stretched almost to his ears as he put his arm around Nandita. He had already met her when he received her at the bus stand but that was for a short time.

Nandita began to show him the new ornaments she had brought from the city—frosted pine cones, sprigs of holly and little Santa Claus figures. 'Tomorrow Alpu and I will go and collect some real cones and decorate them the way we've always done,' she said enthusiastically. 'Nothing can replace the real thing.'

Alpana smiled as she watched them. The thought of not being able to see her parents for such a long time seemed unbearable to her. But Didi was grown up. Old enough to work for her living and live alone in a big city. As Papa and Nandita exchanged old jokes, an odd thought floated into her mind. Had Nandita opened her cupboard and checked out her treasures? Suppose something had got spoilt while she was away? Eaten up by insects the way one of Mamma's shawls was one year, or with fungus like those shoes of Papa's that he didn't wear for a long time. She hoped not. It would be terrible to return and find something precious ruined.

The festive mood permeated the house so thoroughly that dinner turned into a feast. All of Nandita's favourite dishes had been cooked—*kofta* curry, tender green peas, spicy potatoes with puris and caramel custard for dessert.

'How wonderful it is to be home! Thanks so much, Mum, for the good food,' Nandita said in a dreamy voice as she finished the last spoonful of pudding. She leaned back contentedly and said, 'Haven't eaten so well in a long, long time.'

'Glad you enjoyed it,' Mamma said softly. She looked pleased, or was it relieved? Alpana wasn't sure. What with all the excitement and the yummy dinner, she was so sleepy that all she could think of was bed.

'Good night, Didi , Mamma, Papa . . .' She kissed everyone drowsily. But as she was heading towards her room, she thought she heard Nandita whisper to Papa, 'There . . . there's something I want to tell you, Papa—in private . . .'

Alpana's eyes widened. What could it be? She knew there were matters her sister shared only with her father. No problem with that—it was the way things were in their house. Mamma accepted it too. All the same she couldn't help feeling curious. As curious as she still was about the locked cupboard.

On any other morning Alpana would have been tempted to snuggle in her quilt a few minutes longer to escape the freezing air outside it. But the moment she opened her eyes she remembered that Nandita Didi was home. Immediately, she jumped out of bed and rushed to the bathroom.

Brrr . . . how hard it was to brush your teeth when they were chattering! But she had to get ready fast so they could finish decorating the house today. If only Mamma would let her have a go at the cake instead of insisting that she should wait till Christmas Eve. Would she really enjoy it more then? The rich, warm aroma tempted her so much now.

The house was strangely quiet when she stepped out of her room, her new red jacket zipped all the way up. Had she slept that late? No, the clock said it was just half past eight. Papa liked to finish breakfast by nine so they should be at the dining table. But Nandita's door was closed. Maybe she was in the living room. Hmm . . . no one here either. Where was everyone? When she wandered into the dining-room, she found Mamma seated at the table, sipping a cup of tea, all alone.

'Papa had to leave early to attend to a patient,' she said, popping a slice of bread into the toaster. 'And I think Nandita's still sleeping.'

Alpana pulled out a chair silently and sat down. A shaft of sunlight was streaming in through the skylight but the room felt stale and dull today, not bright and merry as it had last night. 'She must be tired,' Mamma continued. Her eyes were a bit puffy as if she hadn't slept too well and the edges of her mouth looked pinched. 'It was a long journey—first on the overnight train, then the four-hour bus ride. Yesterday she was too excited to feel it. Do you want scrambled eggs or an omelette?'

Neither, Alpana wanted to say, but she didn't want to make things more difficult for Mamma. She chewed her toast slowly, hoping that Nandita would suddenly appear at the door calling out, 'Alpu! You're ready! I'll be back in a minute.'

But Nandita didn't appear even after she'd drained her glass of milk.

'Let's go and pick some mustard greens for lunch,' Mamma said, putting down her tea cup. 'Nandita will enjoy the fresh vegetables. And then I need to get back to the Christmas cooking.'

When they got back, Kamla, the maid, told them that Nandita had had her breakfast. Alpana tiptoed to her room. She hoped to find the door open. But it was shut and she could hear her sister talking to someone. Her voice had that tremulous tone which showed that she was upset. Alpana's stomach slid into her shoes.

Something had gone wrong she was convinced . . . but overnight? She remembered the whispered exchange with Papa. No, she was imagining things. Nandita might be talking to someone at work. Maybe she would come out in a minute and say, 'Come along, Alpu, let's go and collect some pine and deodar cones from the forest.'

Nandita did appear, half an hour before lunch. Alpana was putting up wreaths and other decorations in the veranda. She got very restless, just sitting around. Also, she couldn't bear it that the house was looking half done, far from festive. The carol singers would come that night and she wanted to welcome them properly.

She almost jumped when a whiff of perfume wafted to her and turned around with a smile of anticipation. Nandita Didi looked very smart in her navy blue coat and shocking pink scarf. Different, somehow. Alpana had never seen her with so much make-up on.

'Good job, Alpu,' she said. But her face remained blank and her eyes were as opaque as pebbles. Alpana was about to reply when Nandita spoke again. 'Tell Mum that I'm meeting a friend in town and won't have lunch.'

Alpana was dumbstruck. To think they had gone and picked vegetables especially for her. But how would she know? She watched her sister walk away not daring to ask, 'Who, Didi?' She knew all her friends, the ones who had grown up in this town. Most of them had left to take up jobs in the cities or got married.

Mamma just shrugged when she passed on the message. 'You could go and collect the cones yourself,' she said, 'and decorate them, the way you did last year.'

Alpana nodded, though she wanted to yell out, 'But it was supposed to be different this year! We were supposed to do it together!'

'One of Nandita's city friends is here,' Mamma continued, speaking very fast.

'Then why hasn't she invited her here?' Alpana interrupted. 'It's Christmas time. Wouldn't she enjoy doing things with us?'

Mamma sighed. 'It's . . . never mind.' She rose abruptly, leaving her lunch half eaten.

'You're wasting food, Mamma!' Alpana wanted to say. She was seething inside. Why was everyone being so strange and mysterious? Didn't she have a right to know if something was wrong? But she knew if she asked Mamma would say, 'You're a little girl.'

She rose in a fury. She'd go off, take a long, long walk. Take her time coming back. Let them get worried. That would serve them right!

As she went past her sister's room, she noticed the door

slightly ajar. Almost without thinking she opened it and peeped in, as if the key to the mystery lay here. What a mess! Clothes were strewn all over the room, even on the ground. This is why she doesn't let anyone in, she thought irrationally. Then, as usual her eyes found their way to the cupboard.

Her heartbeat stopped. The lock was hanging open.

She stood there for several minutes, rooted to the spot. A terrible roaring filled her ears as her thoughts clawed at each other violently. Should she? Should she not . . . There was no one around. Didi had gone, would be away for some time. Mamma was busy frying samosas. Why shouldn't she take a look? Why did Nandita Didi always shut her out? Why had she let her down today? Maybe she should find out what was in there. It could be important.

Her hands trembled as she opened the cupboard. A faint odour came out of it, the musty smell of rooms long kept shut, mingled with the sharp scent of lavender. Her breath came quick as she stared at the contents. Nothing that mysterious, or valuable . . . Saris hung in straight rows inside and flat bundles wrapped in muslin were neatly stacked on the shelves. So many saris? Nandita hardly ever wore them. She would put one on for church on Christmas day but rarely otherwise.

As she gazed at the saris mystified, realization hit her on the head, hard. The saris looked old, not only old but also old-fashioned. Alpana's head swam. Now she knew why Nandita always kept the cupboard locked.

She felt slightly sick, embarrassed too, as if she had chanced upon someone naked in the bathroom. Why did she have to pry?

Hadn't she known somewhere what the cupboard contained? She could well believe how valuable it was for Nandita. Though it still didn't really explain why Didi shut her out.

She wanted to run away now. Hastily she closed the cupboard and hung the lock back. As she was leaving, her eye fell on a blue velvet-covered box lying on the bed. It looked old too and the lid was half open. Before she averted her gaze Alpana noticed a loop of glossy pearls hanging out, sort of creamy white in colour. She had seen enough, however. She didn't want to explore any further.

Nandita returned just half an hour before Papa did and vanished into her room.

Papa entered the house slowly, with feet that dragged with exhaustion. The line on his forehead didn't go away when he smiled at Alpana. 'I must say the house is looking really nice,' he said, like a visitor making a polite comment. 'Well done, my dear.'

Nandita didn't come out to greet him. She appeared only when the clock struck eight. They had an early dinner, since the carol singers were coming at nine. And it was one of the most miserable meals Alpana had ever had. Because Papa seemed to be pretending that Nandita was not there sitting at the table and she as if Papa was invisible.

How thankful Alpana was when the carol singers came! At least the festive feeling was restored during the time they were there and Papa and Nandita acted normal for a while.

The carol singers left at a quarter to ten after feasting on cake, samosas, *gajar ka halwa* and drinking plenty of hot sweet tea to keep them warm. The moment they did, Nandita turned on her heel and made for her room. Papa gazed at her back helplessly. *What is wrong with both you silly people?* Alpana wanted to cry. She glanced at Mamma. Why couldn't she explain at least? The expression on Mamma's face turned her into a lump of ice. She looked furious. And her eyes were shooting sparks at Papa!

Alpana couldn't bear it any longer. She fled to her room and cried herself to sleep.

She woke up with a slight headache and didn't want to get out of bed. The idea of another miserable day ahead was unbearable. And the day after was Christmas Eve . . .

Today even Mamma wasn't there at breakfast, something unbelievable. Even Kamla's round, smiling face sagged with gloom. Should she take off to her best friend Binny's house? Only, she would have to explain why she was not spending time with her sister. Eventually she took a book and sat in the gazebo behind the house, struggling to concentrate.

Probably she dozed off, because she awoke with a start when she heard Mamma calling out to her. To her surprise Nandita was already seated at the dining table when she got there. 'Where have you been, Alpu?' she said, her voice as tinkly as breaking glass. 'I was looking for you.'

'Reading,' Alpana said shortly, helping herself to rice and dal.

'Shall we collect some more cones after lunch? Some holly, too, perhaps. We can arrange them on the mantelpiece. And if we can find some mistletoe . . .' Nandita's voice quivered suddenly.

'OK.' Alpana wished she could force herself to sound enthusiastic. But too much had happened, was happening. Now she just wanted this Christmas to slip into the past like a bad dream.

Once they were picking their way down the slope, however, her mood changed. Like a chameleon Nandita Didi changed, too, after they left the house. She transformed back into her old self, cracking jokes, tickling Alpana. All the same, the thought that this was just temporary reprieve simmered at the back of Alpana's head.

The sun was losing its warmth when they returned to the house. As Alpana put a foot on the veranda steps, the sound of loud voices jolted her to a halt. It was Papa and Mamma.

'Why are you determined to ruin everyone's Christmas?' Alpana had never heard Mamma speak so angrily to Papa. 'Your daughter's come home after a year and a half and all you can do—'

'She's the one who's ruining it!' Papa sounded even more furious.

'No, it's you! Give her a chance. She's an adult now and can decide who she wants to marry. It's her life. You let her go and stay in the city by herself and now you don't trust her judgement.'

Nandita let out a sound, something between a sob and a gasp. Alpana's skin suddenly felt too tight for her body. She couldn't breathe or move.

'Don't talk about her judgement!' Papa's voice was as jagged as a saw. 'I can't let her throw herself away on any old person. If it were Alpana in her place, would you offer the same advice?'

The silence squeezed Alpana's throat like a noose. Then Mamma replied slowly, 'If it were Alpana? I'd do the same . . . I can write it down and sign it . . . if it would convince you. What a fool I am! I should have stayed out of this and let you ruin your relationship with your daughter.'

Alpana flung down the bag she was carrying. She couldn't bear to hear any more. 'It's no use!' she cried. 'No use even trying to celebrate Christmas! No one cares for anybody else in this house!'

She ran to her room and bolted the door. She wasn't sure how long she had been lying there when Nandita came and knocked, 'Open the door, Alpu,' she said gently, 'Please, open it. It's all right. Everything is all right now.'

'No! It can't be!' Alpana screamed back. 'Leave me alone. I don't want to talk to anyone!'

Mamma came and knocked too, and finally Papa. His voice sounded so sad that a few minutes after he left, Alpana decided to come out.

The house was bursting with cheer on Christmas Eve, the day they exchanged gifts. Miss Kumar who used to teach Alpana in class five was there as usual as was old Mr Roberts who always dressed up as Santa Claus, along with Binny and her parents. There was someone new too, a short and somewhat chubby young man with a ready smile. Nandita introduced him as, 'My friend Samir.'

There was the usual oohing and aahing when the gifts were opened, followed by thanking and hugging. But when Mamma opened Nandita's gift she couldn't speak for several seconds. 'This . . . this is too much, Nandita,' she said finally, in a choked voice.

'No, it isn't,' Nandita said firmly. 'I want you to have it, Mamma.' Her eyes held Mamma's for a long moment and . . . there was unusual warmth in them.

The string of pearls looked vaguely familiar, but it was hard for Alpana to be absolutely sure. Only when Papa cleared his throat and rubbed an eye sneakily that she knew she had guessed right.

The Story that Never Grows Old

Sangeeta Basu

Rosy had finished telling her story. The evening had settled around them like a mystery—hazy with smog. Out here, in the garden, it was cold and three children huddled closer to the glowing coals inside the old, iron cylinder. For a minute or two no one spoke. Then, Pico said, 'I don't believe a word of that. You're just making up a whole lot of lies.' Rosy looked at the two younger children. 'And *you*?' she asked. 'Do *you* think it's lies?' Nikki and Roy looked uncomfortable. After all, Pico was older than they were. He knew such a lot and he always came first in class. Roy was quiet, but Nikki said, 'I don't know, but I *want* it to be true.' Pico began to laugh. He got up and said rudely, 'It's TOSH! You could not have met Santa Claus, Rosy, because Santa Claus isn't real—everyone knows that.'

If you ever met Rosy, you would think that she was a hundred years old. Her shining grey hair was neatly tied into a bun. Her body was stooping and shapeless. She shuffled when she walked. Her face had a million wrinkles criss-crossing all over it. But her eyes always twinkled, and whenever Pico or Nikki rang the doorbell she opened the door and greeted them with a smile that put sunshine to shame. And on evenings like this, when Roy's parents were out and work in the kitchen had been done, Rosy came strolling out to find the children in the garden because she was full of stories to tell.

School had closed for Christmas and Nikki and Roy didn't want to waste a minute of the holidays. They were in the garage at the back of Nikki's garden. It was an old, empty room. There was no car in it—only wooden crates and cardboard boxes and swinging cobwebs. They were making plans: a Christmas tree in the corner; lots of shining candles; crackers to pull; fruit cake, orange juice, sandwiches and chips; crepe paper chains, holly wreaths, and lots of tinsel, glinting. Then, there were cards to write for who they would ask to their party. And, of course, presents for each other. That was the most exciting bit of all. They got busy cleaning out the old garage and making lists of things to buy.

The street where they lived was a mixed up place of houses, old and spreading trees that lined the footpaths, lanes that twisted around and shot off into the neighbourhood behind, small shops that sold all kinds of things, street lamps that threw yellow patterns against walls, and many different families that had known each other for years. Pico and Nikki had been born in the house on the left of the big park, and their friend, Roy, had come to live in the house further down the street when he was two years old and his parents had moved here. Rosy had come with them.

'Only ten days for Christmas, Ma!' Nikki shouted this morning. 'Can we go and buy a tree today?'

'I suppose so,' said his mother. 'Though, why you need to have a tree I can't imagine—you and Pico will have your Christmas fun at Roy's house like you always do.' 'Oh, it's much more fun to have our own party in the garage. And Rosy said she would help us.' 'Mind you don't bother Rosy too much, you kids; she's old and she's not been well. If I hear you ordering her around, you'll get it from me. Understand?'

'Pico called Rosy a liar,' said Nikki, glancing at his older brother. Mother looked at Pico sternly, her eyebrows raised. 'What? She did lie. She said she met Santa Claus.' 'I don't care what she said. You will apologize, Pico. That's no way to

talk to someone who's old enough to be your grandmother.'
Pico scowled.

All the neighbourhood children had gathered in the big park. Aunty Cynthia had arranged it as she did every year. This year, though, she had a surprise waiting for the neighbourhood children. The first thing she did was to make two groups. Pico went to the group for older children. Nikki and Roy were in the group for the younger ones. There were five in Pico's group and about thirteen in Roy's. They all had five days now to think about what Aunty Cynthia had said. From the older children's group, they had to choose someone to dress as Santa and the others would be reindeer. The younger children would all dress like elves and fairies and be Santa's helpers. Together, they had to collect old things from their neighbours and wrap them up beautifully to make gifts. Then, they had to go out on the street and look for the children who lived on the footpath or in the slum close by and give away the gifts. They felt really excited! This was something new! Much better than the plays and songs and fairs they had every year. 'Who's going to be Santa?' Aunty Cynthia asked. Pico's hand shot up in a second and Pico it was. 'Here, Roy! Go tell Rosy that I AM SANTA!' he laughed. 'It's me she met. Tell her.'

Pico was a good leader. He quickly set all the children to work and in the next five days, their street was bustling with all kinds of activity and shouts and yells. They collected old clothes, shoes, blankets, sheets and pillows, toys, books, pencils and crayons. Biscuits and spare cakes were put into separate plastic bags. Soap and washing powder and all kinds of other things joined the lot. It was all stored in the old garage and the children met there every day to get all the gift bags ready.

Rosy came along to help. She was quick with her hands and worked hard, quietly. When the children left, she stayed behind and changed the old, empty room with beautiful decorations that she made by hand. She dressed the Christmas tree and when Pico came into the garage the next morning, he stood gaping. The place was sparkling. The tree was shining with stars and bells and tinsel and green and red holly leaves. A manger stood in the corner covered with straw. Old toys were the Baby Jesus, Mary and Joseph. The Three Wise Men were there, too, and little animals stood all around. She had made a snowman with cotton wool and put it near the entrance with Merry Christmas hanging from his hands.

That evening was the last day of work. Everything had been put in place. Pico's Santa costume was ready and he had a big bell to ring. The reindeer had their brown costumes on and their big antlers on a cardboard ring around their head. The sled stood ready in the garden. All the elves and fairies had come in to try on their dresses and suits and wings and caps. Everyone was eagerly looking forward to Christmas Eve when they would go off onto the street and give away the gift bags.

Pico cross-checked everything one last time and just as he was going to close the door of the garage, Rosy appeared.

'Pico, wait!' she called out. Pico looked up.

'Nikki and Roy are going to have their party here, aren't they?' she asked. 'I guess so,' said Pico. 'I don't really know—they're just kids and I can't be bothered!' 'I was wondering, Pico, since you are Santa, could you allow the slum children and those children on the street across the road to come to the party?' Pico stared at her. He couldn't think of anything to say. 'Wouldn't it be nice to see them playing and laughing and eating together with all of you, for once?'

Christmas Eve was here. It was a gorgeous day. The air was dry and dusty. A winter nip had caught the street. The sky looked a pale blue with cotton wool spirals of cloud drifting off somewhere. The trees were playing with a fitful breeze that pinched your face with cold fingers. It seemed as if the world was waiting for something wonderful, something exciting to happen.

Pico was missing. No one could find him that morning and his mother was beginning to feel annoyed. 'It's very naughty of him to go off like this without telling me,' she said. 'He might be Santa, but he's in trouble when he gets back.'

And where was Pico? He had gone off to find the children across the street first, and then the children who lived in the slum not far off with whom he had played cricket once or twice. For the first time in his thirteeen years, Pico sat with them in their footpath homes, or went into their tiny one-room houses to invite them to the party. He had told no one. Something in Rosy's voice, last evening, had made him think. He wanted to be alone and to understand what Rosy was trying to tell him. And when he met the children today, he knew. He had never noticed them before because he never knew how they lived. Today was different and he suddenly wanted all children in the world to become his friends. He felt a warm, soft feeling rushing through him as he came home and he thought to himself, 'this is what it feels like to love everyone, everyone.'

His mother looked hard at him, straight into his eyes. She had been ready to punish him but after he had spoken she put her hand on his shoulder and said, 'Rosy wasn't lying, you know, Pico. There's a little bit of Santa Claus in all of us. And if you can believe the Santa in you, just for today, you will have changed this world a little. Remember that.'

What their street was waiting for happened like magic on Christmas Eve. The sled came sailing out from the church corner. The reindeer jingled along and pulled it forward slowly and smoothly. Santa, fat in his woolly red costume and cap, rang his bell and shouted out Merry Christmas every now and then. The fairies and the elves came along behind, singing all their favourite Christmas Carols that they had practised so hard every evening in the garage. All the neighbours were out, watching and clapping, and many passers-by stopped to join in the fun.

And then there were the gift bags. Aunty Cynthia had taken them to the garage and put them all around the Christmas Tree. Rosy was there, waiting with the children who had come to the party. She was telling them a story about how she had met Santa Claus. And when Pico walked into the room, with his bell ringing and a ho-ho-ho, his reindeer and elves and fairies with him, you should have heard the yelling and the laughter and the cheers.

It was late when they all went off to their different homes. Pico had not felt so happy in his life. This was the best party he had ever had. He called out to Nikki and Roy. 'You two, help me to clean up or Ma will yell at us.'

Rosy shuffled up. 'Come on then, Santa, I'll help too.' Pico smiled. 'No, you sit here, Rosy and watch us. And, I have a present for you.' Rosy opened the sparkling wrapper to find a lovely little silk scarf and Pico said to her, 'I got it with my own pocket money this morning.'

'But you laughed at Rosy and said she told lies,' said Nikki. 'We thought you didn't like her anymore.' 'I've met Santa too,' Pico said quietly. 'He's real. Rosy knows him very well.' Rosy looked up at him and smiled her sunshine smile. 'I'm glad you've met him too,' she said softly.

'Did you ever go to school, Rosy?' Pico asked. She shook her head, pursed up her lips and said, 'Not one single day in my life!' Pico thought to himself, isn't that strange? She knows more than any of us.

A Wish

Ani Sengupta

Tony lived with his mother in a chawl in a suburb of Mumbai. Like most of them in the city, this one too was falling apart, but its residents didn't care about the peeling paint, or cracked walls, and water leaking from the roof every rainy season. Tony pretended not to care either, but deep down he had hoped he would grow up and move with his mother to a nice apartment where he would have his own bathroom and not share one with his neighbours.

At four feet two inches, Tony was one of the shorter boys in seventh grade but one of the fastest runners and a proficient artist. Like his mother, he had deep set brown eyes, a wheatish complexion and straight black hair, oiled and neatly parted on the left.

Sometimes, on weekends, he would stand in the floor's common veranda and call out to his neighbours to play cricket. Rarely would anyone answer and at times he would hear them snickering and chuckling as they ran down the stairs with cricket bats and equipment. It was only when they were short of a player that Tony would be invited. He often wondered if it was because he didn't have a cricket bat or any equipment of his own.

His good friend and next-door neighbour Rishi was a genius at science and mathematics but lacked any sports skills. All attempts to teach him had failed miserably, so Tony gave up and went fishing with him instead. They would walk to the nearby lake and dig out earthworms from the muddy bank for bait over a hook tied to a nylon thread. An old shuttlecock tied close to the hook acted as a float and kept the thread from sinking.

On one such weekend of fishing, Tony and Rishi returned from their expedition empty-handed again.

'We never catch any big fish,' Tony said to his mother.

'Maybe you don't wish it with all your heart,' she said.

'What do you mean?'

'If you really wish for something from your heart, you'll get it.'

'Then why don't you wish that we get a lot of money?'

'And why do we need a lot of money?' she asked.

'So I could buy a cricket bat. Or maybe we can leave this place and go somewhere far away where we can have our own house, a pet dog and really *friendly* friends for me.'

His mother laughed. 'I wish for your health and happiness, son, and if that requires money then that will come, too.'

'It hasn't come yet!' mumbled Tony. 'Mummy, can I get a cricket set for Christmas?'

'Just borrow a bat from someone when you have to play. You can buy a nice shirt and a pair of pants. See how you are outgrowing them so quickly,'

'I don't want any clothes.'

'Are you sure?'

Tony looked away, not wanting to tell her how he had tried to borrow cricket equipment but in vain. How he had tried playing with the others in the chawl but they wouldn't take him. His mother, too, knew why he went fishing all the time, but his education was getting expensive by the day and she wanted to save for it.

That evening, after dinner, Tony lay on his bed next to the kitchen area and watched his mother wash the dishes. He wondered how she had the patience and energy to cook for him, clean the house, work and take care of him—and, most importantly, never complain.

'Mummy, what would make you happy this Christmas?' he asked.

She continued wiping the plates and answered after a pause.

'Once when you were little, your father organized a

Christmas party in the chawl and everyone contributed to buy some decorations for the old Christmas tree downstairs. We used cotton for snow, crepe papers of different colours, little trinklets hanging from the branches . . . it all seemed so festive. And we had these expensive fireworks, those that emit different colours in the sky. I wish we could do that again.'

'Maybe you don't wish it from your heart,' teased Tony.

'Maybe. You see, I spend *all* my wishes on you,' she said, smiling.

The next day, after school Tony stopped by a store to find out about the fireworks. But when the shopkeeper told him their price, he quickly shied away.

'Too much!' he said to the shopkeeper.

'Yes, *baba*. Everything has become quite expensive and I'm giving you the best price in the market. Do you want any?'

Tony shook his head and left. The only things he could afford were five packets of cotton-wool and three boxes of crepe paper.

On the way home he wondered if he should run errands for the dada in the chawl. That way he could make some money, but his Mother would be upset. Even if he worked in an office or restaurant, she would start nagging that she wasn't able to provide for him and that she should perhaps find another job that pays more. She had never let Tony work during vacations either. Instead, she asked him to run errands and visit a local library so he would read books on science and history and build on his general knowledge in exchange for a paltry sum of pocket money. No matter what he did, she would find out and be disturbed so Tony gave up on that thought.

A week went by and Tony almost forgot about the fireworks. He was about to leave from school one afternoon when Father Joseph, the school principal called for him.

'There's a district level drawing competition in church next week,' said Father Joseph. 'You are so good at it and I think you should represent the school.'

'But Father, I don't have any brushes or paints.'

'Don't worry. They will provide it to you.'

'I'm not sure, Father.'

'If you win, you'll get two thousand rupees, a plaque and a certificate.'

'TWO THOUSAND RUPEES!' exclaimed Tony.

'Yes.'

Tony nodded excitedly and made a mental note of the date and time. As soon as he reached home, he blurted out to his mother about the competition and how he would win the prize money and make her proud. She smiled seeing his excitement.

'What about brushes and paints?' she asked.

'I only need to carry a pencil and eraser,' he said.

Father Joseph had been right about the competition. Tony was amazed at the brushes of all sizes and different colours in little bottles for each contestant. Greens, reds, blues and even gold and silver colours. He had always used white and black to make shades and it was the first time he saw bottles of different shades of the same colour.

Tony drew a bright white *haveli* with a terrace overlooking a lake, just like he had imagined his future house to be. Green coconut trees all around it. On the lake was a boat with white and blue stripes and two boys sitting in it. One of them was holding a large fish while the other one pulled at his fishing rod, ripples forming around its string in water. There were hills in the backdrop and a bright yellow and orange sun peeping from behind them with a few birds flying across the horizon.

When it was done, Tony pinned the somewhat dry painting to the wall like everyone else and wrote his name on the bottom right corner. Then he waited patiently for the judges to make their rounds.

One of the paintings on the wall caught his attention. It was a colourful collage of children playing at a *mela*. It was so well done that it almost looked like a photograph from afar. Suddenly, Tony felt nervous.

'What if I don't win the prize?' he thought.

All the excitement he had felt in the past few days disappeared instantly.

Four judges arrived at his painting, two serious-looking women who didn't smile at all and two men who spent a few seconds looking at it, ready to move on to the next one. Tony tried peeping into their scoring sheets, but they were quick to hide it. The process of scoring continued for another hour and Tony kept thinking about the prize.

When the judges returned to the stage, one of the women took the microphone and praised everyone's artistic talent and effort they had put in. She said she had never seen such a wide variety of ideas. Then the other stern-looking woman took the microphone and spoke about art and its importance in everyone's life. Tony waited patiently as the woman spoke, barely listening to what she was saying. He felt anxious and excited at the same time, wanting to leave with the prize before the shops closed. It was Christmas the next day.

Finally, one of the men whispered something in the speaker's ear and she nodded.

'And now for the results,' said one of the men unfolding a sheet of paper. 'We have only three prizes and it was a very tough competition. We had a very hard time trying to decide, and we scored each painting based on imagination, use of colours, technique and neatness.'

Tony mentally scored his own painting on the criteria mentioned. He thought it was imaginative and neatly done but he hadn't used too many colours. And technique . . . he wasn't quite sure what that was!

'The third prize goes to Tony Pereira!' announced the man.

Everyone in the auditorium applauded as Tony walked to the stage. The man shook his hand and presented him with a certificate but no money. Tony smiled, and thanked him as he accepted the certificate and then stood next to him. The second place went to a boy who had painted a colourful still-life with shadows and textures. He received a silver cup and a certificate. The first place went to the painting of children playing at a *mela*.

'Is that a certificate?' asked Tony's mother excitedly when he returned home sulking.

He nodded.

'I am so proud of you,' she said and hugged him.

'I didn't get the first place, so I didn't get any money.'

'But you came third in the district. That's a very big achievement. I am so proud of you'

Tony threw the certificate on the divan and it flew up fluttering and then settled down.

'Don't be like that. Go look inside that box,' she said pointing to a carton next to their old TV that worked sporadically.

The carton looked old and torn with a shabby red print all over. The upper flaps were open and Tony parted them to look inside.

'Where did you get this?' asked Tony. 'Look there are *anaars* and rockets. Even the ones that burst with colours in the sky. And there are so many of them.'

'I got it from our company,' Mummy said. 'They had some extra boxes and the boss asked me to bring them for you.

Then his mother opened the cupboard and pulled out a long packet wrapped in shiny red and green paper.

'Your Uncle Nestor stopped by this afternoon and brought you this for Christmas,' she said.

Tony could tell it was a little heavy when his mother held it with both hands. He wondered if it were a keyboard since his Uncle was very fond of playing the instrument. Before he could guess any more, he tore away the wrapping paper and opened the box. Inside it lay his first seasoned bat.

Tony hugged his mother in excitement and ran out to tell Rishi.

After an early dinner that evening, he went from door to door telling everyone in the chawl about the fireworks display that would take place next evening. He then asked Rishi to help him decorate the Christmas tree in the courtyard. Together, they threw little pieces of cotton over its branches and stuck coloured crepe paper around the trunk. Mrs Cynthia Egbert, his mother's friend, gave them strings of tiny green lights, which they promptly hung all over the tree.

Next evening, everyone gathered on the veranda to watch Tony's fireworks show. He and Rishi alternated rockets and *anaars* in a line, making sure there was ample distance between them and waited for a go-ahead from his mother.

The rockets lit the sky with fluorescent colours: red, green, yellow, a rainbow and some even made multiple patterns with stars and whirls. Everyone cheered and Tony noticed that his mother was staring into the sky, her face lighting up with every firework. It seemed like she wouldn't stop smiling.

After the rockets were done, he and Rishi continued with *anaars* and *chakris*. The other boys from the chawl gathered around them when his mother walked up to him and whispered in his ears, 'Tony, why don't you share your firecrackers with the other?'

Tony shook his head vehemently.

'Christmas is all about sharing and having fun together isn't it?' she reminded him.

Reluctantly, he invited the other boys to help with the fireworks. They happily took turns to place *anaars* and *chakris* on the ground and light them. Soon, they were backslapping Tony and laughing away like old friends. By the end of the show, one of them asked him if he wanted to join them for a cricket match against their rival chawl the next day. Tony nodded and said that he would bring his new seasoned bat.

The Night before Christmas

Roopa Pai

'I wish we celebrated Christmas,' moaned Kiran, gazing longingly at the plastic fir trees decorated with shining balls and sprayed with fake snow in the shop windows.

'Me too,' agreed Alifiyah. 'Then we could give each other presents and Santa would bring us plenty more.'

The girls began to walk homewards. Their school, St Mary's Convent (English Medium, Regd.), had just closed for the Christmas vacation. Ten glorious days of fun stretched before them, but they seemed a little empty without a Santa.

'We could have collected money for a chawl Christmas

tree, just like we do for Ganpati every year,' said Alifiyah. 'If only Eid hadn't gone so horribly wrong . . .'

Kiran nodded. For the last three months, since Eid, their building, Shakti Chawl, in which Hindus and Muslims had always lived together as good neighbours, had been split right down the middle. The issue was this—when the Eid procession was passing the chawl, someone had shouted something rude. A scuffle had quickly broken out between the Muslims in the procession and the Hindu bystanders. Now the Hindus and Muslims in the chawl did not speak to one another.

As they neared the chawl, the girls waved and went their separate ways. It wouldn't do for them to be seen walking in together.

For the next five days, the girls moped around their homes, getting more and more irritable. What good were holidays if you were not allowed to spend them with your best friend?

Finally, on Christmas Eve, Alifiyah's Ammi sat her down, exasperated. 'What is the matter with you?' she said. 'I know you're missing Kiran, and I'm really sorry, but there's nothing I can do about it. I miss Kusum too, you know.'

Alifiyah knew. Kiran's Aai and her Ammi were best friends, just like she and Kiran were. She even knew Ammi could do nothing about what had happened. But she was still angry. 'I just think it's stupid!' she fumed. 'All Kiran and I wanted was to have a little Christmas tree . . .' She burst into tears.

'Oh, *kaleja*, don't cry,' soothed Ammi. Then her eyes lit up. 'Tell you what, if it is only a Christmas tree that you want, I'm sure I can help you.'

'No, you can't!' cried Alifiyah. 'They are too expensive.'

'Not that one,' said Ammi, pointing to a fledgling coconut tree in the chawl compound.

'Ammi, what kind of Christmas tree is that?' sobbed Alifiyah.

'The kind that was around baby Jesus on the very first Christmas,' said her mother. 'Remember he was born in a desert! So maybe there were date palms around him, not coconut palms, but this is close enough . . .'

Alifiyah considered. Ammi was right. And Santa would understand. 'What about decorations?' she said, beginning to get excited.

'Well, I have a few balloons and streamers somewhere . . .' began Ammi, pulling a plastic bag off the topmost shelf.

'And Kiran has lots of silver and gold foil left over from our school project!'

Before Ammi could stop her, Alifiyah had rushed out into the corridor. 'Kiran! Come down to the coconut tree! Bring all the foil!'

In a trice, the girls were downstairs. They wrapped the streamers around the little trunk and draped them over the leaves. Then they began to blow up the balloons. Soon a small group of chawl kids had gathered around.

'We need something to wrap the foil around,' said Kiran.

'I've got some old ping-pong balls!' said Rafiq, the chawl's

TT champion. 'They are a little squashed, but once you have covered them, they'll be fine.' He raced off to get them.

'You need a drill to put a hole through them,' said Khalid, 'so that you can string them up and hang them.' He went off to find his dad.

'Khalid!' called Sarla Didi, who had been enjoying all the action from her ground floor room. 'Bring an extension cord, too! I'll get our Diwali lights.'

Alifiyah and Kiran looked at each other and grinned. They had really started something here! Then the same thought jumped into both their heads. The crib! Just before school closed, their class had been taken to the chapel to see the Nativity scene—baby Jesus in the manger, sheep and cows around him, shepherds, the Three Wise Men on their camels . . .

'Get all your toy animals,' Kiran said to the little ones standing around.

'Can I get my Spiderman?' asked a boy.

'Of course! Sarla Didi, can we have some string, too?'

Soon, with every boy and girl in the chawl helping out, the one-of-a-kind Shakti Chawl Christmas Coconut tree was ready. Little silver and gold balls twinkled from in between streamers and balloons. Camels, elephants, dinosaurs, cows, cars, trucks, and a motley array of action figures—most of them with one or more limbs missing—hung lopsidedly from the leaves or stood below the tree. The Diwali lights winked on-off, on-off, in every colour of the rainbow. Everyone came out on to their balconies to cheer the kids.

'Now all we need is a baby Jesus!' clapped Kiran.

'I know!' said Guddi. 'Remember my doll? The one that was baby Krishna at Janmashtami? He will be perfect!'

'No way, dum-dum!' needled Raju the bully. 'Jesus was fair and blond, he wasn't a darkie like your ugly doll!'

'For your information,' interjected Alifiyah snootily. 'Jesus was born in Arabia, where the sun is very hot and people have brown skin and black hair.'

All the children snickered. Guddi dashed out of her home with the doll, and raced towards the tree. Then, suddenly, she stopped short. Two men were blocking her path—Mahesh Babu, the big dada of the chawl on the Hindu side, and Hanif Mian, the mean-eyed leader of the Muslim side.

'What is this nonsense going on, henh?' demanded Mahesh Babu, his eyes darting fire as he turned on the scared group near the tree.

'Khalid, Rafiq, back to your homes, now, or I'll take your skin off!' growled Hanif Mian. 'Who gave you permission to play with those kids?'

A couple of little kids began to cry. A few others began to slink away. Then a clear, high voice rang out from one of the balconies. 'I did!'

It was Alifiyah's Ammi. Hanif Mian looked up, furious. 'I gave them permission, Hanif Bhai,' said Ammi, looking straight at him, fearless. 'It is enough, all this fighting. We don't even know what we're fighting about anymore.'

'I agree!' Another voice, from two floors above. It was Kiran's Aai.

'And I!' said someone else. 'And I!' 'And I!' 'It is enough!'

In the chaos, Guddi slipped past the two men to the tree, and placed the doll in Sarla Didi's fruit basket. 'I'll get my ammi's hijab to cover him,' whispered Khalid. 'The bright pink one with the glittery sequins.'

Once baby Jesus was all wrapped up, Alifiyah and Kiran looked around a little nervously to see if anyone had noticed. But nobody was paying them any attention any more. They were too busy laughing and chatting, catching up with friends they hadn't spoken to in three months. There was no sign of Mahesh Babu or Hanif Mian.

'Isn't our tree beautiful?' sighed Kiran.

'The most beautiful in the world!' agreed Alifiyah. 'Hey, the book in the library says we should put out cookies for Santa!'

'Pah!' snorted Aai. 'I bet Santa is sick of cookies. Just put out six of my *besan laddoos*!'

'Good idea! But do you think he will really come?'

'I don't see why not!' said Ammi, and she nudged Aai, giggling.

A Song that Lives On

Swapna Dutta

The year was 1818. Joseph Mohr, pastor of the St. Nicholas Church in Oberndorf, a small village near Salzburg, Austria, stood by the window watching the Salzach River. It was Christmas Eve and bitterly cold outside. The river often flooded its banks in spates of fury. But this time, the recent floods would affect their Christmas celebrations like never before. It looked like the church organ—the only one in the village—was not working and would not be able to provide the music so essential for the choir. What was he to do about the Midnight Mass?

Emil, a young man who helped him with his work, came inside the room. Mohr looked up anxiously, 'No hope, Emil?'

'None, Father. We can't get a note out of it.'

'You don't think it's because of mice chewing up the bellows like the last time? Or is it because of the rusting caused by the mildew? The Salzach has had so many floods this year . . .'

'It's most likely the mildew, Father. The sound had been going from bad to worse and now there's no sound at all. What are we to do about the music tonight? Isn't there any chance of getting hold of Herr Mauracher?'

Karl Mauracher, from Zuegen, Zillertal, in Tyrol was the master organ builder who travelled all over Austria repairing faulty organs. He had been called to their small village for repairing the organ several times before. But Zillertal was far away.

'You know there isn't,' said Mohr pacing up and down the room, 'Christmas would be over long before he even got to hear about our organ. I'll have to think of something else, and God will be on our side. Don't worry, Emil. We shall have music for our Midnight Mass.'

An idea had occurred to Mohr while standing by the window. He had been thinking of trying a new composition for the Mass sometime this year. He remembered a poem he had composed two years ago, when he was the assistant pastor in Mariapfarr. But then, he had fallen so ill that he had to be hospitalized in Salzburg.

Just before his illness he had been on a solitary walk and had looked down on the tranquil village from a hilltop. It made him think of the first Christmas and how the angels had announced the birth of the long-awaited Messiah to the shepherds on a hillside. He had written the poem soon after. He wondered now if that poem could be turned into a song. It was a simple song befitting Christmas Eve and could be sung to the accompaniment of the guitar that he often played himself. *And* he had a friend who was a musician and composer!

It was still dusk when Mohr set out in the bitter cold to walk to the neighbouring town of Arnsdorf where his friend Franz Gruber lived. He was a schoolteacher but he was also the choirmaster and the church organist. Like Mohr, Gruber had also studied music. Gruber was surprised to see Mohr at this time.

'Franz, I must ask a favour of you,' said Mohr, 'I have a poem that I wrote two years ago. I want you to put it to music right now so that we can have it for the Midnight Mass tonight.'

'So soon?' asked Gruber amazed.

'We have no time to lose,' said Mohr, 'Please compose the melody suitable for two solo voices that can be sung to the accompaniment of the guitar. You know our organ isn't working. The choir can provide the harmony. They must learn it right away.'

'And the song?' asked Gruber.

'You and I must sing it,' said Mohr, looking at him.

The friends got busy. Gruber composed the melody for the carol with guitar accompaniment in just a few hours, and had time to rehearse it with the church choir. The choir was very excited and put their heart and soul into the new music. What was most important, they had managed to learn it in the short time!

That night the congregation at the Midnight Mass in St. Nicholas Church listened enthralled to an exquisite carol—*Stille Nacht! Heilige Nacht* (Silent Night, Holy Night)—for the first time as Mohr and Gruber sang the song together to the accompaniment of Mohr's guitar. The choir repeated the last two lines in four-part harmony. And thus a new song was born that was to find its way into the hearts of millions of people throughout the world. But that was for the future!

The song might have remained confined to the little Austrian village had it not been for the same damaged organ once again. Karl Mauracher made several trips to Oberndorf to repair the organ until he decided to replace it with a new one in 1825—seven years after this incident. While working on the organ he heard the story of the new carol *Silent Night* and asked for a copy of the music. Mohr had already been transferred to a different parish in another town by then. But Mauracher managed to find a copy and took it back to Tyrol with him.

Those were the days of travelling folk singers, very like the Von Trapp Family Singers in *The Sound of Music*. Mauracher passed on the new song to two such travelling singer families whom he knew—the Strassers and the Rainers. Both groups included the new song in their repertoire eagerly. It has been recorded that the Strasser Family Singers sang the carol in a concert in Leipzig in December 1832. They changed the notes of the song a little. And theirs is the version we know today.

The Rainer Family Singers also presented the song in their programmes. According to a historical plaque, the Rainer Family sang the Christmas carol before an audience which also included Emperor Franz I and Tsar Alexander I. Gradually the carol became known throughout the region and, in 1834 the Strassers performed it for King Frederick William IV of Prussia. The king was so impressed that he asked his cathedral choir to sing it every Christmas.

In the year 1839, the Rainers performed *Stille Nacht* for the first time in America at the Alexander Hamilton Monument, outside Trinity Church in New York City. By the turn of the century, the carol was known in England, New Zealand, Africa, and the Americas and gradually, in all the other continents. Christian Missionaries carried it with them wherever they went.

Mohr served in a number of different parishes after being transferred from Oberndorf. In 1838, he was appointed pastor in the Alpine village of Wagrain where he served until his death on 4 December, 1848. Throughout his life he remained a humble priest and died totally penniless because he had donated whatever he had earned to be used for the education of children and care for the elderly in his area. He was described by the bishop as 'a reliable friend of mankind, toward the poor, a gentle, helping father.'

By the time his carol became really famous, Mohr was

no more and no one remembered who had composed the music. Although Gruber wrote to the music authorities in Berlin telling them that he had composed the music for the popular carol there was no way that he could prove it. The musical world assumed that the song must be the work of Mozart, Haydn or Beethoven who were the greatest music composers of the time.

This assumption continued until the twentieth century and people forgot all about Gruber. The controversy was finally put to rest in 1994, when a long lost arrangement of 'Stille Nacht, Heilige Nacht' in the handwriting of Joseph Mohr was authenticated. Mohr had written, 'Melodie von Fr. Xav. Gruber' in the upper right-hand corner. A letter written by Mohr was also found where he had stated that his collaboration with Franz Gruber to produce *Silent Night* on 24 December 1818, was one of the best times in his life, adding, '*The two of us did something for the Holy Night. I transcribed the words and Franz Gruber the melodie.*'

During his lifetime Gruber produced a number of orchestral arrangements of his composition. The original guitar arrangement is missing, but five other Gruber manuscripts of the carol still exist. The manuscript by Joseph Mohr dated 1820 is for guitar accompaniment and is probably the closest to the arrangement and melody sung at the Midnight Mass in 1818.

There is another incident related to the song that took place during the next century. The year was 1914. World War I was raging and had already claimed more than ten million lives. Soldiers on both sides of the battlefield somewhere in France were facing a dark and frozen Christmas Eve. They were mostly young men, longing for their home and family.

Suddenly some soldiers on the German line placed candles on small branches and raised them above their trenches. It touched the hearts of everyone, including their enemies. Thousands of soldiers on both sides started singing Christmas carols. What had started so spontaneously in those moments became the legendary Christmas Truce. Weapons were put down and the soldiers came out of the trenches to gather in no-man's-land to celebrate Christmas.

So, for a short period of time, no shots were fired. The next day, the soldiers who had fought fiercely only hours before, stood side by side and buried their dead comrades, holding a brief service afterwards. But before they left to go back to another freezing night in the trenches, a solitary voice broke out into *Silent Night* in French. He was joined by another voice—but this one sang it in German, the words known and beloved by both sides. By then, *Silent Night* was nearly a hundred years old.

Speaking of the true 'miracle' of *Silent Night*, Christmas historian Bill Egan says, 'The words flowed from the imagination of a modest curate. The music was composed by a musician who was not known outside his village. There was no celebrity to sing at its world premiere. Yet its powerful message of heavenly peace has crossed all borders and language barriers, conquering the hearts of people everywhere.'

The Best Christmas

Rituparna Chatterjee

Ralph rolled down the window of the brick red car and stuck his head out, inhaling the crisp winter air. His twin sister Ralphina did likewise, popping her head out. They smiled and closed their eyes. The refreshing mountain air helped iron out some of their motion sickness and fatigue. They had flown from Mumbai to Guwahati. This drive—from Guwahati to Shillong— up the winding roads with needle-sharp turns lurking at corners, was the last leg in their long journey from their home city of Mumbai to their grandmother's house in Shillong.

The twins were ten years old though Ralph insisted on his superiority, being all of 16 minutes older. It had been three years since the Crawford twins had visited Shillong. They were now jogging their memories to remember whatever little they could from their visit as toddlers. It was their own private little jigsaw puzzle game: fitting in what they saw around them with pieces of what they imagined were past memories.

The emerald fields down the slopes were blending into a lush forest cover of pine and pear. The groves draped the mountains like a thick magical carpet in various hues of green. The famous clouds of Meghalaya had descended to have a picnic. They shrouded the tops of the mountains and the trees, making them look like a long headless army standing still awaiting orders. Somewhere amidst these, tumbling waterfalls and randomly babbling brooks appeared and disappeared. Drizzles and mist kept wafting in and out of whimsical pockets, so you never knew what was ahead of you until you went really close and the view or the objects decided to finally say, 'Oh all right!' and showed themselves.

'It's all like a magical land,' remarked Ralphina. 'Just like it was then,' retorted Ralph. And it might as well have been except for the vehicles honking past every now and then.

'Hey look, there's Umiam Lake,' screamed Ralph, pointing at every lake they approached. 'Not!' intercepted Ralphina each time, smartly pointing out the signboards bearing the correct names.

'Look! That's Shillong Peak, where Nana had taken us for that wonderful picnic,' said Ralph excitedly through his binoculars, pointing to a peak in the distance. 'I was seven, but being older, naturally I have a better memory. 'Not!' said

Ralphina quickly. 'Not not!' said Ralph a few seconds later as the fog lifted to reveal the signboard.

The closer Ralph and Ralphina got to the heart of the city, the more convinced they were that everything was the same. In the Barabazar market, the local Khasi women sold oranges, pears, wildflowers, medicinal herbs and all kinds of Christmas ornaments and goodies, while their ruddy-cheeked babies, wrapped up on their backs, peered curiously from behind. Chatty children from the many boarding schools roamed the market in their school blazers. The air was abuzz with the promise of the approaching festivities.

'I wonder if Nana's house still looks the same,' said Ralph. 'You will find out soon. We are almost there,' said their driver Sukhwinder Kaka.

'I'm a bit nervous, Ralph,' said Ralphina.

'What? You were jumping with excitement all the way. Why so nervous now?' said Ralph.

'Well, we have been here just once and that too with Mommy and Daddy,' said Ralphina. 'This time it's just the two of us. And we have to be on our best behaviour. You never know with Nana. She isn't like other grandmas.'

Their mother Rina's aunt was indeed no ordinary woman. She was almost 70 years old but beneath her wrinkled papery skin, were the muscles of a tough mountain girl. She insisted on doing much of the household work in her 100-year-old house by herself. She painted the walls herself and fixed many an odd job for which one would normally call the electrician or the plumber. During their last visit, she had fixed a leaking flush, a blocked sink and a fuse. She embodied 'Work is Worship' and made sure that others around her did as well.

Nana was affectionate but did not spoil them silly or lovingly overlook their faults like other grandmothers. If they wanted something, she ensured that they worked for it and took responsibility.

'Remember the last time you wanted brownies in the middle of the night?' quipped Ralphina.

'Yes, she made me bake them!' whined Ralph.

'But hey, it was so much fun!' Ralphina reminded him.

'And when we wanted pears, she took us to the orchard and made us climb trees to pick out pears of our choice,' whined Ralph. 'Even though, we could have had it delivered from the market or the gardener would have got them off the tree.

'Do you remember his two kids and the baby?' said Ralphina.

'Yeah, whatever! I'm tired' said Ralph.

'So says the frail almighty older brother!' quipped Ralphina, sticking out her tongue to tease him.

The car entered the driveway, flanked by Nana's enormous garden, and parked at the house's door. Sukhwinder Kaka removed the luggage and the twins got out. 'There she is!'

whispered Ralph. 'I hope work doesn't await us yet. I want to relax after the long journey.'

'You try to act so big,' said Ralphina. 'But you really are a baby. From today your name is Baby Relaxo.'

'And yours is Sister Meano,' said Ralph with a smirk.

'Well, hello there, children,' said their grandmother emerging from the flower garden with scissors in her gloved hands, a floppy hat on her head and gardening shoes. 'How lovely it is to see you, my darlings!' she said, hugging them tightly. 'I almost didn't recognize you. You are so big now! You can actually help with the garden, too.'

'I'd love to, Nana,' Ralphina said, nudging Ralph. 'Ralph was especially eager to clean the chimney so that Santa can have a clean entry.'

'That's wonderful, Ralph!' said Nana.

'Woof woof!' said someone. And when they turned, that someone jumped all over them, drowning them with kisses. It was Nana's humungous furry Bernese Mountain Dog, Burly Bernie. When they had last met him, he had been barely a few weeks old and had just entered their grandmother's life. But from all of his jumping and hurling himself over people half his size, it was clear that he still thought of himself as a puppy and was completely unaware of his size.

Arm-in-arm and laughing and jumping, the twins and their grandmother and Burly Bernie entered the big house where brownies and milk awaited them.

Chewing on his umpteenth brownie, Ralph looked out of the window and saw a bunch of kids of assorted sizes. They were picking up dry leaves in the garden. 'Hey look, there they are. That must be them,' Ralph said, nudging his sister. 'They probably are Shibulal's kids,' he said, recalling the gardener's name.

'Ah! Yes, now what were their names?' said Ralphina.

'Being older than you, I clearly remember that it was something Aaloo,' said Ralph.

'Don't be silly!'

'Yes, yes that's what it was,' said Ralph. 'They are Aaloo, Kaloo and baby Bhaloo.'

'Haha, yes, in the zoo. Not here,' said Ralphina.

'Let's go find out,' said Ralph. 'If I win, you'll ensure that I don't get another electric go-kart or another PSP bundle for Christmas,' said Ralph.

'And if you're wrong, then you have to absolutely make sure that I don't get another dumb princess dress or another Barbie in a castle,' said Ralphina.

'It's a deal!' they chorused and shook hands to seal the agreement and walked up to the kids.

'Hello!' said Ralph.

'Ah! You're back,' said the tallest of the trio, who appeared to be about 14 years old. 'City brats . . . I remember the last time you were here,' he muttered.

'Hey, that's no way to welcome anybody,' scowled Ralphina. 'So much for mountain hospitality.'

'What was it that we did that was so bad?' asked Ralph. 'We were just seven . . .'

'You created such a ruckus,' the boy said. 'Our folks had to work extra time cleaning up after you and tending to your tantrums. It ruined our Diwali.'

'You were always cribbing about everything,' said the mid-sized girl, who appeared to be ten years old. 'And always scowling. I don't understand why. You guys have everything,'

'We did no such thing; at least I don't remember' said Ralph. He turned to the smallest one. 'And you, little girl, what do you have to accuse us of?' The toddler grinned back innocently.

'Hey! Leave Shalu alone, you rich bully,' said the big boy.

'See I told you, Ralph,' said Ralphina, smiling. 'You were wrong. Now you owe me a Barbie-free Christmas.'

'Huh!' exclaimed the big boy wondering what had gone wrong.

'We had a bet,' explained Ralphina. 'He thought your names were Aaloo, Kaloo and Bhaloo and I said they're not.'

'Who is named those things?' asked the big boy. 'What are we poor folks to you, clowns? It's Malu and Shalu . . . You guys are mean.' He looked angry, but wise enough to not pick up a fight. 'Let's go, sisters,' he said, and they trooped away behind him.

The twins felt bad. They had not meant to be snooty or rude. 'Hey! Wait,' called out Ralphina running behind the trio. 'I am . . . we are, really sorry! It's not like that. Please, we're really sorry!'

'Yes, we didn't mean it,' repeated Ralph.

'It's OK, Bhaiyya,' urged Malu. 'They don't even know they are spoilt. And they seem genuinely sorry.'

'Yes, Bhaiyya!' said Shalu, who didn't understand much of the older world but loved to repeat everything that she could.

'Oh, all right!' said Balu.

'Friends?' said Ralphina, extending a hand.

'Okay!' said Balu.

'Yes!' beamed Malu.

'Yesh!' grinned Shalu.

'Well, why don't you show us around?' said Ralphina. 'We city folks don't really know much about the mountains.'

'But whatever we have seen, we totally love,' added Ralph, not wanting to sound like a city brat.

'There are adventures everywhere you look,' said Malu. 'You just have to look.'

'That's awesome!' said Ralphina. 'Why don't you take us for one?' asked Ralphina.

'I wish I could but I've got work to wrap up,' said Balu, pointing to the baskets of dry leaves. 'And then we have homework to finish.'

'We could help and then you could have extra time before homework to take us for an adventure,' said Ralphina with pleading eyes.

'That sounds perfect!' said Malu.

'Pre-effect!' quipped Shalu.

And so the twins helped gather up the dry leaves and set out. At the gate itself, they had their first adventure. Lines of metal with gaps in between were made in the ground, to trap cattle's hooves and prevent them from entering the property. A bushy tail popped up and down the gaps, as if in a game of hide-and-seek.

The children cautiously crept closer. 'Hush! It might be a mongoose attacking a snake,' said Malu. Balu tore off a thin branch from a tree and tapped it in front of their feet for protection. Turned out that it was just a squirrel—camouflaged with speckles instead of stripes. It's greed for snacking had emboldened it to graze for goodies in spite of humans lurking mere centimetres away.

The children grinned and gleefully hopped down the slope to explore the town.

The twins' grandmother lived right by the ancient church. Built in 1864, the grey stone building was a historic beauty. But today on Christmas Eve, she was decked in her finest. The fresh paint on the rims, the polish of the doors and stained glass windows gleamed in the evening sunlight. A beautiful scene, reenacting the birth of baby Jesus in a manger was created on the side. Soft tones of Christmas carols wafted out. Come sunset, the myriad star lanterns and colourful vines of Christmas lights wrapped all over the church would light up, making it look like it was out of a fairy tale.

Downtown, Christmas Eve celebrations were in full swing. People were starting to head home to dress up for the

Midnight Mass, a few hours later. But before that, they had a dozen errands to run, and hundreds of things to be ticked off their shopping lists. Christmas carols like *Silent Night*, *White Christmas*, *Rudolph* and of course *Jingle Bells* poured out of the speakers in the shops. Barabazaar was in a frenzy. The youngsters roamed around in groups, munching on steaming momos and sipping on hot beverages to keep themselves warm on the cold December night. Many of them excitedly discussed the famous Shillong Chamber Choir, which was just about to start their Christmas performance. Nobody could escape the festive air. Even the stray dogs sported fake mistletoe collars around their necks.

It was dark when they headed back. They crossed a series of small dilapidated houses. The cracked foggy windows of the houses revealed the humble life of their residents. Families huddled together around lanterns and little *sigris*, or pots of hot charcoal embers, rubbing their hands for warmth, eating out of thick worn-out utensils. A few of them had bowed their heads, probably in prayer. Others sat together singing melodies, often accompanied by local stringed instruments. But what struck the Crawford twins especially, even from so far, was the joy on their faces.

They were home. Shalu, Malu and Balu lived with their parents in their quarters on the property itself. 'See you on Christmas. Goodnight!' they said to one aother and vanished into their respective homes.

'How did my darlings like Shillong?' asked Nana. 'Did you have a good walk? My, my, you kids look serious. Why don't you have a hot shower? Then you can eat dinner and we can all head for Midnight Mass?'

'Nana? May I ask you something?' said Ralph.

'Yes, my child,' she said.

'How can people have so little and be so happy?' asked Ralph. He narrated what he had just seen and asked Nana what the secret was.

'Haha, my lovelies. You can have a perfectly happy Christmas with very little. The secret is sharing,' said Nana.

'Should I tell you the story of my best Christmas?'

'Yes please, Nana!' begged the twins, eager for a story.

'It was when I was a teenager. My father owned a theatre called The Ambassador. It was the only theatre in Shillong at the time, and a fairly grand one at that. All the wonderful Hollywood stars—Charlie Chaplin, Greta Garbo, Katherine Hepburn—came alive on its screens. Every Saturday, the town people gathered there, dressed in their finest, to watch the latest film. Youngsters liked to come in half an hour or so before the movie to hang out. There was an ice cream parlour with a jukebox, a fat red popcorn machine and mechanical vending machines which would dispense bubblegum, when fed with coins.

'Where is it Nana? How come we haven't seen it?' asked Ralph.

'Oh Nana, I want to see it, too,' begged Ralphina.

'Alas, my darlings. The Ambassador is no more. We saw some bad times and ultimately, Father was forced to sell it off. The new general store you see now in Barabazaar with all the imported goods, that's where The Ambassador once was,' said the twins' grandmother.

'Then what happened?' said Ralphina snuggling close to Nana.

'The Ambassador was all we had and our last night—before we lost it to Munshilal, the new buyer—happened to be Christmas Eve. We had a gorgeous theatre and a ton of popcorn. So guess what we did?' asked Nana, rolling her eyes mischievously towards her grandchildren.

'What? What? I have no idea!' said Ralph.

'We stayed up for hours sewing popcorn together into garlands and wrapped them around the pear trees outside the theatre. And we alternated each one with ribbons of pink and blue candyfloss. We had not one but four Christmas trees. And they were the most beautiful trees in the world.'

'Wo-ow!' said Ralphina dreamily.

'And we sat there spending our last night together having no idea what we would do the next day,' said Nana softly. 'We knew we'd soon be poor without The Ambassador. And yet we decided to be merry: drinking port wine and hot chocolate and eating plum cake, mince pies and roast chicken. We knew that it would be our last fine meal in many years. The best Christmas gifts are often invisible ones . . . like that year we had togetherness, family, faith and hope—all of which helped us battle what could have been our darkest night. But it turned out to be the most magical Christmas we ever had. After several years of hard work, we became comfortable again. We had many cosy Christmases, but none like the last Christmas at The Ambassador.'

The children sat quietly imagining the scene, thinking about Nana's story.

'All right,' she said. 'Hurry up and get dressed now. It's almost time for the Midnight Mass.'

They got ready and walked to the glowing church down the slope. Burly Bernie too tailed along, greeting his furry street friends.

When they returned, they were exhausted. Burly Bernie settled by the fireplace while Nana tucked the children in bed.

Nana woke up at 5am on Christmas morning, and went to the kitchen to heat up the kettle, which was the first thing she did every dawn. She had told the children many times to not be wasteful. And yet, she could tell from the light seeping in through the gap between the bedroom door and the floor, that the kids—who had probably woken up in the middle of the night—had left the lights on.

And then, something on the floor caught her eye. It looked as if it were a string of short puffy white flowers, right at the edge of her bed. Getting rather curious, Nana grabbed her glasses to get a better look. She held a piece in her thin hand and lifted it close to her eye for inspection. She rolled it among her callused fingers, and smelled it. Could it really be? Was it? It was indeed, of all the things in the world, not some kind of a flower, but popcorn!

Holding it gently, she used the fragile popcorn rope as a guide, to see where it took her.

It went on across the floor and took her straight to the Christmas tree, adjacent to the fireplace. The popcorn garland strung itself all around the Christmas tree, zigzagging its path across the ornaments.

'Someone must have put a lot of thought, love and labour into this,' thought Nana. There, beside the tree, along with the huge wrapped up presents, were her precious grandchildren along with Shalu, Malu and Balu.

They were huddled together like a bunch of tired sleeping puppies. In the glow from the dying fire, they looked like angels. Next to Balu, was an old tin with an assortment of needles and spools of thread. Packets of microwavable popcorn lay strewn around.

Nana was extremely touched. 'Awww, my angels!' she said. They had recreated her favourite Christmas for her! And Shibulal's kids had joined in to help in the middle of the night. She did not want to wake them up, but was so beside herself with joy that she could not help herself hugging them.

They awoke slowly rubbing their sleepy eyes.

'Oh Nana, did you like it?' asked Ralph eagerly.

'It was all my idea to sew the popcorn garlands, Nana,' said Ralphina proudly.

'But you could not have done it without us, City Girl,' said Balu. 'You did not even know how to thread a needle!'

'As if you know how to sew, Balu,' Malu came to Ralphina's defence. 'Dadi, I taught them to sew. Can you see what a horrible job they have done! They don't know knots. We just had to use Fevicol to glue things together. Can you imagine, Dadi! And here I am a seamstress-in-the-making. How shameful!

'But whose bright idea was it to use Fevicol, when we couldn't sew one endless string?' said Ralph. 'None of you could have thought of it.'

'But I'm the tallest and the strongest,' boasted Balu, not wanting to be left out. 'Only I could get all that Act II popcorn from the top kitchen shelf

Little Shalu somehow managed to stay asleep throughout all the commotion.

'Right, right my lovelies, you are all so wonderful.' said the grandmother. 'But let me fix you some hot cocoa first. And some Yule Log, especially for Shalu, Balu and Malu.'

'Really, Dadi?' said Balu. 'Yuuuum!' said Malu.

'Of course! I'll get the kettle ready. Call your parents, Malu. I don't want them to shout at you or get worried that you are missing,' said Nana, hugging Malu. 'We will all sit together and then you can tell me all about what you did last night. But before that I must thank you. This takes me back to my best Christmas!'

Ralph and Ralphina nodded. Their own best Christmas had just begun.

Little Piccola's Christmas Surprise

Retold by Urvashi Bahuguna

Once upon a time there lived a little girl called Piccola who grew up in a small stone cottage deep inside the sunny woods of Southern France. Although Piccola lived in a bright and sunny land, her life was quite hard, yet she never complained. Her father had died when she was a baby and she and her mother lived all by themselves far away from other people. So Piccola had no friends of her age and only had her mother for company. And her mother was not around most of the time as she had to make a living for the both of them by gathering flowers, fruit and firewood from the forest.

Every few days, she would gather her collected stuff and make her way to the nearest village and sell it there. Now the village was nearly a whole day's walk and Piccola's mother was not so young anymore. So she couldn't go there often enough and the money her produce earned was insufficient for their needs. At the best of times, Piccola and her mother would have some hard bread and fruits plucked off trees. Needless to say, little Piccola had no dolls or toys and had never laid eyes on a book.

But despite not having much, Piccola wasn't an unhappy child. She loved wandering through the forest, climbing the trees and wading in the nearby stream. There was one tree in particular that she liked to climb. She would scramble up to its highest branch and sit there for hours, staring at the stream and watching the birds that stopped at the water for a drink. On her way home, she would always pluck some wild flowers to brighten up their simple home. Although their one-roomed house was simple and bare, Piccola and her mother made sure that it was always clean. The sun generously filled the room with light, and it was a small but happy place.

One summer, a woodcutter and his family built a house close to where Piccola and her mother lived. He had four children who spent their time running about the garden and dancing and singing and playing games. Piccola would look at them from afar, curious but shy. Piccola's mother noticed her daughter's interest in their neighbours and one evening when she returned from the forest, she took Piccola along for a visit. The woodcutter and his family were delighted to have company.

The wife told them, 'Piccola should come and play with the children. They keep themselves amused and busy all day with games.'

And so from that day on, Piccola would spend nearly every day roaming around the woods with the other children. She took them to all her secret hideouts and showed them how to climb trees and skip stones over water. In turn, they shared with Piccola the few books they had, and she was introduced to stories and worlds she could never have imagined. The only stories Piccola knew were the ones her mother told her before bed every night. One of Piccola's favorite stories was the story of St. Nicholas' secret descent through the chimney and the gifts he would quietly leave in people's stockings. The night before Christmas, her mother would tell her the story right before putting her to bed. On Christmas morning, there would be a surprise waiting for her in her stocking. Piccola was usually too excited to sleep and would be up at the crack of dawn.

Piccola helped her mother knit stockings every Christmas so that St. Nicholas could leave them gifts. But one Christmas, things were particularly bad and there was nothing to eat in the house. In desperation, Piccola's mother sold their stockings so that they could buy bread for a Christmas Eve dinner. Piccola walked to the village with her mother to sell their stockings. She observed the holly wreaths that hung from people's doors and the smells that drifted out from their kitchens. Through their windows she saw Christmas trees with a star or an angel on top and with a small pile of presents beneath. Piccola had never seen a proper Christmas celebration before. Her eyes grew wide in wonder, and she asked her mother if they could make a wreath that Christmas. They gathered holly leaves on their way home and using spare string fashioned a wreath to hang on their front door.

When Piccola passed the woodcutter's home, she saw the whole family gathered around the fireplace hanging stockings on the hearth. Even though their Christmas was simple like Piccola and her mother's, they still had stockings and a warm fire. Piccola was dismayed, but did not have the heart to let her mother see it. She was worried that St. Nicholas would have nowhere to leave her gifts now. She feared he would come and not finding a stocking would have to leave without giving Piccola and her mother presents on Christmas.

Piccola sank into gloom at the thought. But just when all seemed lost, she remembered her wooden shoes. Piccola had one pair of shoes and though her feet were cold without them, she took one off and placed it near the hearth. They were the closest things Piccola had to stockings and she believed in her heart that St. Nicholas would understand and leave her present inside the shoes. Her mother saw what her daughter had done and said to her sadly but gently, 'Don't think of Christmas this year, my dear. If we have enough to eat, we should be grateful.'

After Piccola had gone to bed, her mother searched the house for something, however small, to put in there so that Piccola did not wake up to an empty shoe. But there was nothing in the house except for a few coins which would have to be kept for bread. Piccola's mother worried all night about the disappointment she knew her child would have to face when she woke up. She decided to wake before Piccola and gather some flowers to place in the shoes. It was the best she could do. She did not want Piccola to lose her faith in Christmas.

A little before dawn, she crept out of the bed she and her daughter shared. She tiptoed lightly out of the room so that she wouldn't wake Piccola. But when she neared the hearth, there was a lovely surprise waiting for her. During the night, a little sparrow had flown in through the window they always left open for air. Cold and looking for a corner to snuggle into, the sparrow had settled into Piccola's little shoe. The shoe was just the right size for the bird, and warm and cozy. After a long night of looking for somewhere to rest, the sparrow had flown in and fallen asleep. The mother could barely contain her excitement and ran to wake Piccola to show her what Christmas morning had brought her.

'Piccola! Piccola! Look! Come, see what St. Nicholas has left you.' Piccola, rubbing her eyes, got out of bed and went into the next room. Piccola bent down to stroke the bird, and just as she touched the bird, it's wing shivered and it gave a tiny cry of pain. Piccola and her mother realized that the bird had hurt its wing. Over the next several days, they nursed the bird back to health. They would crush some of their bread into crumbs for the sparrow, and kept it warm under a small quilt Piccola knit for her. During those winter months, the bird would stay indoors with Piccola and her mother, recovering its strength.

The woodcutter's children couldn't believe Piccola's luck! Though they had received toys and sweets on Christmas, none of that compared to Piccola's new companion. They would often come visit Piccola's house to play with the bird and hear it sing. When springtime came around, and the woods were warm again, Piccola brought the bird to the window and watched it take a few nervous steps before it flew out and successfully managed to take a circle around the house. With Piccola's help, the sparrow had lived to survive the winter.

The bird stayed the entire summer in the nearby woods and would often come perch at their window where there was always a fresh bowl of water and a few bread crumbs waiting for him. With the help of the woodcutter, Piccola and the children built a small birdbath near her cottage. All kinds of birds would stop there for a drink in all seasons. The little sparrow had changed Piccola's life.

And every Christmas Eve since that day, Piccola has slept soundly knowing that St. Nicholas will find a way to make Christmas morning special for her.

All About Christmas

Subhamoy Das

Christmas: the Word, the Date and the Story

The Word

Christmas, which comes from the Old English phrase 'Cristes mæsse', or festival of Christ, is celebrated as the birth of Jesus Christ.

The Date

The Bible doesn't tell us anything about the day or year of Christ's birth. However, it is generally believed that Jesus was born sometime between 7 BC and 4 BC.

About circa 350 AD, 25 December was chosen by Pope Julius I as the date of 'Nativity' or Christ's birthday. This date, which falls close to the winter solstice, was celebrated from very ancient times as the time of winter festivals.

Now, Christmas Day is a public holiday in most countries around the world, including India. It is one of the most enjoyable holidays of the year for children, as they believe that Santa Claus will come with bags full of Christmas presents for them.

The Nativity Story

The Nativity dates back to more than 2000 years ago in the town of Nazareth in Israel. Once there lived a young woman called Mary, who was engaged to be married to a carpenter called Joseph. One day, the angel Gabriel appeared before Mary and said that she would soon become the mother of a very special baby and that she should name him Jesus.

Soon after the couple were married, and Mary was due to have her baby, the Roman Emperor Augustus passed a decree whereby all Jews had to get themselves registered in their place of birth. Thus Mary and Joseph had to go on a long and difficult journey to Joseph's hometown Bethlehem. When they arrived in Bethlehem, the city was so crowded that Mary and Joseph could not find any place to spend the night. Finally, a generous innkeeper allowed them to stay in his stable for the night. This is where Mary gave birth to her son a few hours later. As there was no bed for the baby, she wrapped him in cloth and laid him in a manger filled with hay to keep him warm.

At the time of Jesus's birth, some shepherds near a hillside in Bethlehem, saw a bright light appear in the sky. It was an angel sent by God to share the good news about the birth of Jesus in Bethlehem. Hearing this auspicious news, the shepherds went to see the baby. As they arrived at the stable, they were filled with divine joy and knelt down to pray to baby Jesus. They told Mary and Joseph the story of the angel and revealed that Jesus was no ordinary boy, but the son of God.

The Three Wise Men

Soon after the birth of Jesus, three wise astrologers in a faraway land, saw a new star shining bright in the sky. They knew this was an indication that a great King of Jews was born and set out to find the baby. Now King Herod, the existing ruler of Jews, grew very worried on hearing the prophecy of the wise men. He then asked the Three Wise Men to go find the baby and let him know so that he could offer his respects to this divine child. Guided by the bright star, the wise men made their way to Bethlehem.

Once there, the Three Wise Men, also called the Magi, knelt down and worshipped Jesus. The Magi left the baby gifts of gold, frankincense and myrrh. That night as they slept, all the three men had the same dream where an angel appeared and warned them that King Herod wanted to kill baby Jesus. The next morning when they awoke, they decided not to return to Herod's palace and advised Joseph to leave Bethlehem and escape to Egypt where Jesus would be safe.

All About Santa Claus

The Name and the Look

That jolly old man with white beard and a flowing red suit and big sack of goodies is every child's favourite thing about Christmas. This beaming 'Father Christmas' is no modern day invention and has been around for a century or two.

The name 'Santa Claus' comes from the 4th century Greek gift-giver and miracle-maker, St. Nicholas or Sint Nikolaas/Sinterklaas as pronounced by the Dutch, who brought this fantastic tradition to North America.

The characterization of Santa Claus has many different influences. However, the most vivid description of Santa Claus appears in Clement Clarke Moore's Christmas poem for children—*A Visit from St. Nicholas* written in 1823.

Inspired by Moore's poem, Thomas Nast, a famous American cartoonist came up with a caricature of Santa Claus, which gave the merry old man, his physical attributes which continue till today. And so was born the burly grandfather-like character with red and white fur-lined clothes and hat. Nast's version of Santa brought to life some popular myths and curious traditions. It gave Santa a home near the North Pole and a mode of transport—a sleigh pulled by eight flying reindeers including Rudolph, the red-nosed reindeer, and sometimes followed by a number of magical elves. Along with Santa and his reindeers came the custom of filling up stockings with presents on the night of the Christmas Eve and the idea of Santa secretly entering homes through the chimney at night.

Haddon Sundblom, an American commercial artist first drew Santa in a red suit trimmed with white, with black boots and a black belt which were used by the Coca Cola Company in its advertisements in the 1930s.

Today, this mythical figure is one of the most loved characters and is well known all over the world. In England, Santa's name is Father Christmas; in France, he is known as Pere Noel; in Germany, he is called Christindl or Christ Child; in the Netherlands, he is Kerstman; in Finland, Joulupukki; and in China, Santa Claus is called Shengdan Laoren.

The Legend of Saint Nicholas

Nicholas was born in the 4th century AD to a rich Christian family in Patara, a place near Myra in Turkey. He traveled far and wide and was very kind and pious. He was known for his helpful nature and good deeds, which finally resulted in his appointment as the Bishop of Myra.

It is believed that St. Nicholas travelled anonymously in the night to check if the people in his area were happy and healthy. During one of his nightly visits, he heard a poor family crying about their misfortunes and how the father was forced to sell his daughters as slaves to save them from abject poverty. That night, St. Nicholas secretly threw three purses of gold through the chimney into their house and saved them from distress.

As his popularity grew throughout Europe, and especially in Holland, he came to be regarded as the protector and the patron saint of children and sailors. Even to this day, St. Nicholas continues to enjoy his reverence and popularity in the form of Father Christmas or Santa Claus.

Santa Claus and his gift-giving tradition continues to be an important part of Christmas festivities across the world. However it is interpreted differently in different countries. In Holland, Santa Claus arrives by boat and a donkey carries his sack of toys. In Italy, the gifts are bought by a good witch who rides on a broomstick. In Sweden, Christmas gifts are bought by a gnome, who rides a sleigh which is pulled by goats. In Australia, Santa Claus has a white beard, wears a red swimsuit and rides on waterskis.

The Real Santa Claus Village and Town

If there's one place on earth that can be called Santa's home, it's got to be in Finland's Lapland region. The Santa Claus village near Rovaniemi in southern Lapland has become the top tourist destination in Finland because of its Santa Claus connection.

This amusement park is popular with both adults and children who visit Lapland throughout the year. Visitors can see Santa's office and his magical grotto where cute little elves will invite you in for a chat with Father Christmas and a photograph with him.

You can also cross the Arctic Circle here, and even send a letter home from Santa's Post Office. Opened in 1985, the Santa Claus Post Office has handled millions of letters with addresses from 197 countries. Here you can choose your Santa Claus postcard and send home Christmas greetings with a unique Santa Claus postmark.

Santa Claus is also the name of a small town in Indiana, United States. This settlement, established by some Americans of German descent, got its unique name in 1852. From its street names to its architectural style, this town has a festive look throughout the year. It also boasts of Santa Claus Land, the world's first theme park, which was built in 1946, nine years before Disneyland.

Many years ago, when the postmaster of the Santa Claus Post Office noticed people sending letters addressed to 'Santa Claus', he decided to answer them himself. Since then, the Post Office at Santa Claus has been processing thousands of letters to and from Santa Claus.

Each Christmas, parents and grandparents drive to Santa Claus, Indiana, to post their personal letters with the only U.S. official Santa Claus postmark to their child or grandchild. This tradition has kept alive the magical belief among children that Santa Claus does really exist in real life and outside of Christmas stories.

Write a Letter to Santa

Children love writing and getting letters from Santa. When kids come to know that Santa would be visiting their home with gifts on Christmas Eve, they write letters to him with their choice of Christmas presents. It is a custom to place letters near the fireplace or on the mantle for Santa to come and read them.

Today, it is actually possible to post a letter or send an email to Santa Claus.

- In Canada, children write to: Santa Claus, the North Pole, Canada, Postcode—H0H 0H0
- Kids in the United States write to Santa Claus, the North Pole, Alaska.
- The British Royal Mail sends letters to Santa at this address: Father Christmas, North Pole, SAN TA1.
- Finnish children write to Santa at: Santa Claus, Santa Claus Village, FIN-96930, Arctic Circle, Finland.
- You too can write to Santa by sending an email at CanadaPost.ca and IGCO.com. And yes, you will get a reply from Santa Claus.

The Christmas Tree

Evergreen plants have been important symbols long before Jesus Christ was born. From the earliest times, people in ancient Egypt, Rome and other parts of Europe worshipped evergreen coniferous trees such as fir, balsam and spruce as representations of life and rebirth. Wreaths and garlands made of these trees were believed to represent everlasting life.

Trees had great spiritual significance in different parts of the world. The Scandinavians decorated their homes with evergreen trees in hope of a good harvest, while the Egyptians brought green date palms into their homes to keep them happy and hopeful through the winter months. The druids in ancient Britain hung the leaves of evergreen plants in doorways to ward off evil spirits and bad luck. The setting up of a Christmas tree at home was thus a part of this long tradition of tree worship.

More specifically however, the tradition has its roots in 16th-century Germany, where people decorated a fir tree with apples to remember Adam and Eve in the Garden of Eden. These were called 'Paradise trees', and they were decorated on Christmas eve. Over time, other baubles and bits such as stars, candles and ornaments were added to it, and the Christmas tree as we know it was born. Legend goes that it was a German called Martin Luther (the leader of the 15th-century Protestant Reformation) who brought the tree indoors. As he was returning home one wintry night, he saw the stars twinkling in the sky through branches of a fir tree. Charmed by the sight, Martin Luther went into the woods and got himself a small fir tree. He then took it indoors and decorated it with candles, which represented the stars he had seen. This custom spread in Germany and then all over the world. The first Christmas tree in England appeared when Queen Victoria married Prince Albert, who was German. In 1841, Albert set up a Christmas tree at Windsor Castle to remind him of his homeland. The first artificial Christmas tree also originated in Germany, in the 19th century, when dyed goose feathers replaced the evergreen leaves.

The Myth

The most beautiful story about the first Christmas tree is associated with the birth of baby Jesus. The night Jesus was born, all living things including men, animals and even trees came to Bethlehem bearing gifts. The olive tree brought its luscious fruits, the palm its best dates. Right at the end of the queue, stood the little fir tree. But it had no gift to offer for it had no sweet fruits or pretty flowers. So all the other big trees pushed the fir tree into a corner.

An angel who was standing nearby felt sorry for the fir tree and commanded a cluster of stars to come and rest on its boughs. When baby Jesus saw the lighted tree he smiled and blessed it and said that henceforth the fir tree would always be decorated with lights during Christmas to please little children. That is how the fir became an integral part of Christmas and was thereafter known as the Christmas tree.

Christmas Decorations

All kinds of decorations are used to brighten up the Christmas tree and the home during this time. The main colours of this festival are red, green and white as well as gold and silver and a variety of decorations are available in all these colours.

The Star

Traditionally, either a star or an angel is placed at the top of the tree. The star represents the Star of Bethlehem which first revealed the news of Christ's birth to the three wise men and then led them to baby Jesus in Bethlehem.

Tinsel

The Christmas tree is often decorated with silvery strips called 'tinsel' which has a legend too. Long ago there was a woman who was so poor that she had no money to decorate the Christmas tree for her children. 'Children,' she told them frankly, 'I am sorry I have nothing to decorate your Christmas tree with and no presents to hang from it either. So, would you rather not have a tree this year?' she said, wiping a tear. 'No, Mother,' they said. 'We will have the Christmas tree as usual even if we have nothing to put on it.' The poor woman prayed that the children might not feel too unhappy about their tree, and someone up there actually heard her prayers.

For that night when they went to sleep, spiders landed up on the bare tree and wove cobwebs all over it. When the children woke in the morning, they saw their tree covered in fine cobwebs which shone like silver in the moonlight. And so tinsel started being used to decorate all Christmas trees.

Holly Leaves

The evergreen holly tree with pretty pointed leaves and clusters of bright red berries is said to represent the life and death of Jesus Christ. The holly is connected to the Crucifixion of Christ and his resultant death, after being tried and sentenced by the Roman prefect Pontius Pilate. The thorny leaves symbolize the crown of thorns that was placed on his head before the Crucifixion. The red berries represent drops of blood that spilled from his wounds when he was nailed to the cross. The evergreen leaves are said to symbolize eternal life and Christ's resurrection from the grave. The name 'holly' probably came from the word 'holy'. It is believed that the holly berries used to be yellow at first. But they turned red when they were stained with the blood of Jesus.

Mistletoe

Mistletoe was used by Druids (Celtic Priests of the pre-Christian era) 200 years before the birth of Christ in their winter celebrations. This plant was worshipped because of its remarkable properties: it had no roots, yet it remained green during the winter months. The ancient Celts also believed mistletoe had magical healing powers and was an antidote for poison and infertility, and kept evil spirits away. The plant was also seen as a symbol of peace, and it was said that among Romans, enemies who met under mistletoe would lay down their weapons and embrace.

Scandinavians associated the plant with Frigga, their Goddess of Love, and it may be from this that the custom of kissing under the mistletoe is derived. It is believed that those who kissed under the mistletoe were blessed with happiness and good luck and possibly a wedding in the following year.

Christmas Traditions

Although, Christmas is deeply rooted in Christian theology, its celebratory vibe and festive traditions have made it a nearly secular festival with all kinds of wonderful little traditions that appeal to people across religions and nations.

Gifts

Christmas has long been associated with the tradition of gifts. Some believe that this practice has its roots in the Magi carrying presents for baby Jesus. Others believe that it was Saint Nicholas' habit of secret gift-giving that the tradition draws inspiration from. Whatever be its roots, the month before Christmas is the biggest shopping season of the year!

Festive Colours

The Christian explanation behind the traditional colors of Christmas is that red symbolizes the sacrifice and the blood of Christ; green represents everlasting life and the evergreen tree that does not shed its leaves throughout winter. Fir trees and holly bushes remain in bloom long after other plants have withered away from the winter cold. Historically the Romans used to make green holly wreaths in winter that would hang from the doors and walls in celebration of the winter solstice.

The Grinch

The Grinch began as a fictional character created by the famous children's author Dr Seuss, and has since become a Christmas icon. Dr Seuss first wrote about him in the story *How the Grinch Stole Christmas*! He is a devious, scheming hater of Christmas and the holiday spirit, whose heart is described as 'two sizes too small'. The world fell in love with the villainous Grinch who was covered in green fur and had terrifying red eyes. His image can be seen everywhere on Christmas collectibles, TV shows, movies and books to do with Christmas.

Christmas Carols

The carol we know today is a song or hymn set to popular music and based on Christmas themes. The songs which started off as hymns were adapted in local languages and set to popular tunes. These easy melodies were then carried by travelling musicians from place to place and house to house thereby starting off the tradition of carolling which exists till this day.

Christmas Cards

Even in this age of emails and mobile phones, post offices around the world get immensely busy during the weeks leading up to Christmas in delivering millions of Christmas cards. As the story goes, in 1843, Sir Henry Cole of England got too busy to write to his friends over the holiday season. Instead, he asked John Horsley to print black and white cards. They were then painted by hand and delivered on Christmas. The rise of the 'Penny Post' postal service in UK in the 1840s furthered this custom of posting greeting cards and gradually the practice of sending Christmas cards became popular the world over. The original design by Horsley was reprinted in 1955 and can still be found today. The traditional message on a Christmas greetings card says, 'Wish you a Merry Christmas and a Happy New Year' or 'Season's Greetings'.

Christmas Dinner

While a whole Roast Turkey, Roast Chicken or Roast Goose continues to be served on English and American tables at Christmas, in warmer Australia, this bird is usually carved up and served cold to give everyone a bit of respite from the summer sun. Originating from ancient sacrificial meats and traditional Christmas feasts, large poultry is the star of the table. In other countries like Austria and the Czech Republic, a giant Fried Carp (tasty freshwater fish) usually competes with the bird. A Brazilian Christmas dinner features a whole lot of porky delights, while Iceland takes the Christmas spirit to a whole new level and has a Roast Reindeer as the centrepiece of the dinner table.

Sweet treats like the Christmas Yule Log (a chocolate cake which is shaped like a log of wood), Christmas Pudding with Brandy Butter, Christmas Cookies, Gingerbread Men, Pannetone (a sweet bread loaf popular in Australia and New Zealand) Christstollen (a German fruit bread) and Mince Pies (sweet treats with minced fruits, spices etc) complete Christmas dinners across the world.

And warm Mulled Wine and Egg Nog keeps the winter chills away.

Fun Festival Activities

Stand Alone Christmas Star

You need:

Printer (optional) • Stiff paper (like card stock, thick chart paper or thin cardboard) or styrofoam trays • Scissors • Crayons or markers

MAKE IT!

1) Two paper stars are needed to make one three-dimensional star. Draw two identical 5-pointed stars of the exact same size on a piece of stiff paper.
2) Cut out the stars, and then decorate them on both sides. If you don't want to decorate them, you can just use coloured paper. The traditional Christmas colours are red and green, you could use one of each.
3) Make one slit in each star. In one star, the slit is through an inner corner between two points till the centre of the star. In the other, the slit through an outer corner till the center.
4) Slip the two stars together through the slits you just cut. For stability, you may have to tape the stars a bit where they meet at the slits.
5) You now have a great three-dimensional star decoration that stands by itself on a table.

Paper Christmas Tree

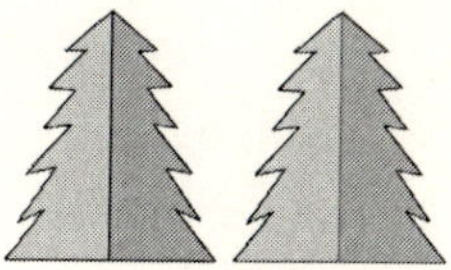

Make a simple three-dimensional Christmas tree from construction paper. These trees look great sitting on the mantle or on a windowsill.

You need:

Green construction paper or chart paper • Crayons, markers, glitter glue, or tempera paint • Scissors • Clear tape • Optional: Other colours of construction paper, glue, hole punch, stickers

MAKE IT!

1) Fold a piece of green construction paper in half and then cut it in half.
2) Place the two pieces one on top of another, and fold them in half again.
3) Draw half a Christmas tree on either side along the fold.
4) Unfold the papers, and cut out the outline of a tree.
5) Fold the papers in half again, this time horizontally in order to mark the center of the tree. Mark this with a pencil.
6) On one tree, make a slit from the top of the tree running through the middle till the centre. On the other, make

the slit from the bottom, running through the middle to the centre.

7) Slip the two trees together along the slits. Using clear tape, tape the bottoms and tops together (pieces of tape on the bottom and at the top make the tree stand up well and stop the slit ends from flopping over).
8) Decorate your tree with crayons, markers, glitter glue, or tempera paint. Or you can glue on tiny construction paper decorations or use star stickers. You can cut out tiny paper balls using a hole punch.Now you have a really nice 3-dimensional Christmas decoration.

Christmas Tree Sun Catcher

You need:

Green Construction Paper • Coloured Tissue Paper • Glue

MAKE IT!

1) Cut a Christmas tree shape out of the construction paper. Use a hole puncher and punch out holes all over the tree. Glue coloured tissue paper to cover the holes you punched.
2) Use brown paper and cut the shape of the trunk. Place a

star sticker on the top and glue the trunk to the bottom of the tree.

3) You could colour ornaments and garlands with crayons. To personalise the tree, you could cut out the first letter of your name and stick it on the tree.
4) Hang in windows for a lovely stained glass look.

Ice Cream Stick Trinket Box

You need:

Glue • Ice cream sticks • Trinkets or seasonal decorations to personalize the box

MAKE IT!

1) First take 2 ice cream sticks and set them about 3 inches apart. Then glue 10 sticks across them.
2) Now flip over the base and begin gluing on ice cream sticks for the walls, alternating between the sides. Continue this till the walls are as high as you like.
3) To make the removable lid, set 2 sticks alongside the last 2 wall sticks and add a line of glue along each one.
4) Now lay 10 ice cream sticks across them.
5) To personalize it, glue a small Santa Claus, a seasonal decoration or a trinket to the top.

Edible Angels

You need:

1 cup peanut butter • 1 cup honey • 2½ cups powdered milk • Waffle cones • Thin liquorice string • Raisins or currants • Coloured gems.

MAKE IT!

1) To make the clay, put peanut butter, honey, and powdered milk in a big bowl.
2) Squeeze and knead the ingredients together. If the clay is too sticky, add a little more powdered milk. If it is too dry, add a little more honey or peanut butter.
3) When you have nice, smooth-feeling clay, shape it into a 3-inch cone to make the angel's body. Add a little ball of clay on top for the angel's head.
4) Carefully break off parts of the waffle cone and press two pieces into the angel's back for wings.
5) Wind some liquorice string around the head for a halo.
6) Stick raisins on the head for eyes and gems on the body for some colour. Your yummy angel is ready to fly into your tummy!

Tissue Paper Wreath

You need:

Paper plate • Glue • Scissors • Red and green tissue paper • A festive bow, preferably in red or gold. If you don't have a bow, you can easily make one from coloured ribbon.

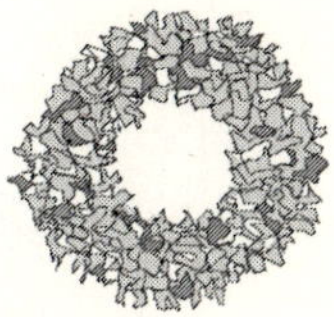

MAKE IT!

1) Cut the tissue paper into 1 to 2 inch squares.
2) Cut the centre out of the paper plate to leave a round 'donut' shape. This will form the base of the wreath.
3) Wrap each square of tissue paper over the top of a pencil so it forms a flower like shape, dip it in glue and stick it to the paper plate.
4) Continue until you have filled the entire plate with tissue to create your wreath.
5) Use mostly green tissue paper with the occasional piece of red to make it look like there were holly berries in the wreath.
6) Stick an ample bow at the bottom centre of the wreath and voila! you have a traditional Christmas wreath. You can hang it on a hook anywhere in your house.

Brown Paper Stocking

Make a great Christmas stocking from a brown paper grocery bag. You can hang it from your mantle and stuff it with Christmas goodies.

You need:

Thick brown paper (like grocery bag paper) or brown felt
• Pencil • Scissors • Glue • A hole puncher
• Yarn • Markers or crayons

MAKE IT!

1) Draw a large stocking on thick brown paper (or brown felt).
2) Cut out two copies of this stocking.
3) Punch holes around the edges of the stocking.
4) Weave yarn in and out of the holes. Leave a loop of yarn at one end, and tie it in a knot.
5) Decorate your stocking with crayons, markers, stickers, construction paper cut-outs, or glitter.

Christmas Charades

You need:

Chits of paper • A pen • A bowl

PLAY IT!

1) Make a list of Christmas-related themes such as names of carols, holiday traditions and popular Christmas movies.
2) Write them down on chits of paper which you place in a bowl.
3) Take turns picking out a chit and acting out the words with gestures while remaining completely silent.

Hand and Foot Reindeer

You need:

Brown and tan (or orange) construction paper • Pencil • Scissors • Glue • Googly eyes (optional)

MAKE IT!

1) Trace around the child's foot using brown construction paper. This will be the reindeer's head.

2) Trace around the child's hands using tan construction paper. These 2 pieces will be the reindeer's antlers.
3) Glue the handprint 'antlers' to the top of the reindeer. Add a bright red paper nose, a paper (or drawn) mouth, and googly eyes (or paper eyes) to the reindeer's head.
4) You can now decorate your house for Christmas with these cute reindeers. Don't forget to put the child's name and age on the back of the reindeer.

Paper Plate Snowman

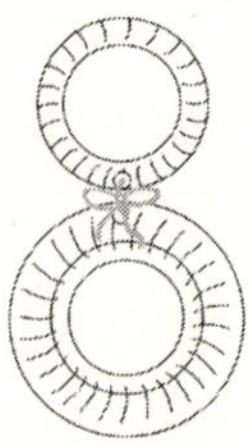

Make a cute snowman decoration using two paper plates. This makes a nice decoration to put on a door or hang in a window

You need:

2 white paper plates • Construction paper (black, red) or wrapping paper • An orange tube or carrot end (for the nose) • A short length of yarn or ribbon • Hole punch • Marker or crayons • Scissors • Glue • Optional: googly eyes, large buttons

MAKE IT!

1) On one of the paper plates, cut off the outer rim, making a smaller plate.
2) Punch a hole near the rim on both plates.
3) Tie the two plates together, using the yarn (or ribbon).
4) On black construction paper, draw and then cut out a top hat and two boots. On coloured construction paper, draw and then cut out two gloves.
5) Glue the hat, boots and gloves on the snowman. Either glue on googly eyes or draw eyes. Draw a mouth. For the nose, cut a short length from an orange tube. Stick the tube through the plate to secure it (if the plate is too tough, make a tiny hole with the tip of the scissors).
6) For the buttons, you can cut out shapes from construction paper, use round stickers, glue on real buttons, or simply draw them.
7) You now have a cute snowman decoration!

Secret Santa

You need:

Chits of paper • Pen

PLAY IT!

1) On each chit, write down the name of one family member/ classmate/friend.

2) Put all the chits together, and have everyone pick one at random. The person whose name they pick out is the one they will give a gift to on Christmas.
3) Make sure the identity of the Santas stays secret.
4) You can put a price limit on the gifts so that it's fair.

Snowman and Elf Christmas Poop!

The perfect Christmas gag for kids with a good dose of potty humour!

You need:

Two pretty glass jars • Green and Red Cadbury's Gems or M&Ms • Any white mint candies • White labels (the kind that has gum at the back or cut white paper into labels and stick with magic tape)

MAKE IT:

1) Fill one jar with green and red Gems or M&Ms and the other one with the white mint.
2) Draw some holly or Christmas trees on the labels and write Elf Droppings and Snowman Poop. You can also make up little poems and write them on the labels . . . For eg:

'Snowman felt hungry and ate too much soup.
His tummy went rumble . . . and here is a jar of his poop.'

'This elf ate too much candy when he went shopping
His face went green . . . and here is a jar of his dropping.'

3) Stick them on to the jars.
4) Gift these poop jars to a friend or keep them around the house for a snack and a smile!

Christmas Star Ornaments

You need:

Ice cream Sticks • Gems, Jewels, Rhinestones, Buttons and Other Decorative Items • Glitter Glue • Fevicol • Paint Brush and Color • Ribbon • Scissors

MAKE IT!

1) Make five-point stars using the craft sticks and glue them together.
2) Paint the star in the desired color and let it dry completely.
3) Shape the loop of a ribbon and glue it at the back of the star, so that you can hang the star ornament on your Christmas tree easily.

4) Glue on beads, buttons, jewels, rhinestones and other assorted items to decorate your stars.
5) You may also use glitter glue to make some of the sparkling stars.

Charity Gift Cartons

You need:

Old cartons • Markers • White tags • Pretty wrapping paper • Long strips of ribbon • Cellotape

DO IT!

1) This Christmas, engage in a little spring cleaning of your house.
2) Put aside all the old books, clothes, toys, utensils, blankets, knick-knacks etc that you have outgrown or never use.
3) Sort these items into different cartons or bags.
4) Label the white tags with names like Toys, Blankets, Clothes etc.
5) Put strips of wrapping paper on top of the cartons to make it look festive.
6) Make bows out of the ribbon and stick them on top.
7) Pack the cartons neatly and stick the tags with cellotape.
8) Find a nearby orphanage, old age home, community center, homeless shelter or charity and drop them off in time for Christmas.

Special Christmas Tree

This community activity can help all the underprivileged children in your neighbourhood share in the Christmas spirit.

You need:

A largish tree preferably an Ashoka (or any other conical tree resembling the approximate shape of a Christmas tree) • A few enthusiastic volunteers • All kinds of baubles, small toys, glittery hairclips, ear rings, ribbons (old and new) • Cotton wool • Lots of white chart paper • Paper Punch

MAKE IT!

1) Seek help from your family, friends and neighbours, the local RWA and collect a bunch of colourful baubles and shiny odds and ends.
2) Call all the kids of the domestic help, drivers, *dhobis* etc in the neighbourhood. Give them spools of coloured thread and cellotape and ask them to attach them to all the baubles.
3) Give them squares of the white chart paper and ask them to fold them and cut random shapes into it.
4) Punch holes and string with thread.
5) Suspend the decorations from your tree.
6) Keep adding more stuff as and when they come along.

7) This tree will bring a lot of cheer to the neighbourhood and make everyone feel Christmassy.

Christmas Tongue Twisters

You need:

Silly Christmas tongue twisters

PLAY IT:

1) Say each phrase three times as fast as you can. Let kids practice on their own or take volunteers to come up and try their best for all to hear. A candy prize for anyone who tries. There are some examples below but you can let your imagination run wild and come up with phrases that your own.
2) Santa sings super songs on starry stairs • Santa skis over snowy slopes to save some time • Big bright bells bring bubbling bags of smiles • Grumpy Grinch gets grizzled and grouchy • Pretty packed presents and poodles in pink • Sally's striped stocking swinging from the sleigh • Santa's super sleigh swiftly slides sideways • Cheery carols with Christmas cookies and candy cane caps.

Popcorn Strings for your Christmas Tree

You need:

A couple of bags of plain popcorn (the plain unbuttered variety) • Some newspaper • Some dried red bora berries or any other red berries available at your local store • A spool of heavy duty thread • A long needle • 2 buttons

MAKE IT!

1) Pop the popcorn and upturn it on sheets of newspaper so that it cools fast. You can pop a few into your mouth while you wait.
2) Thread the needle but don't cut it off at the other end as you need a lot of thread to make a popcorn string that goes around your tree.
3) String popcorn and a dried red berry alternately or in clusters.
4) When you have made a long enough string cut of the end, put a button at either end to hold them in place and tie a knot.
5) Your festive popcorn string is ready to add cheer to your tree.

Christmas Present Hangings

You need:

Empty matchboxes • A couple of sheets of colourful wrapping paper • Clue • Ribbons of ditterent colour

MAKE IT!

1) Wrap the matchboxes in different types of wrapping paper.
2) Tie little bows out of the ribbons with long ends.
3) Stick/staple or tape them on top of the boxes.
4) Use the ends to tie around the branches of your tree.

Christmas Playlist

Check out our list of Top 10 Christmas songs that you can play in the run up to the festival.

All I want for Christmas is My Two Front Teeth—Spike Jones and his City Slickers • Happy Christmas (War is Over)—John Lennon • The Christmas Song—Nat King Cole • Have Yourself a Merry Little Christmas—Judy Garland • O Holy Night—Celine Dion • Santa Claus is

Coming to Town—Bruce Springsteen and Bon Jovi • Jingle Bell Rock—Billy Idol • White Christmas—Bing Crosby • Deck the Halls—Nat King Cole • Silver Bells—Bing Crosby and Carol Richards

The Christmas Movie Marathon

Bring in the festivities with a Christmas movie marathon. We bring you our top 10 Christmas films.

It's a Wonderful Life (1946) • *How the Grinch Stole Christmas* (1966) • *A Christmas Story* (1983) • *The Nightmare before Christmas* (1993) • *The Muppet Christmas Carol* (1992) • *Miracle on 34th Street* (1947) • *Home Alone* (1990) • *The Polar Express* (2004) • *Snowman* (1982) • *Elf* (2003)

Carols

Go Carolling with Friends. Put on your Santa hats. Wrap a green muffler around your neck and pull on a red shirt and sing your hearts out. Go to your friends' homes and put up a little performance and we're sure you'll get lots of sweet treats and applause for your efforts.

1. Jingle Bells

Dashing through the snow
In a one horse open sleigh
O'er the fields we go
Laughing all the way
Bells on bob tails ring
Making spirits bright
What fun it is to laugh and sing
A sleighing song tonight

Oh, jingle bells, jingle bells
Jingle all the way
Oh, what fun it is to ride
In a one horse open sleigh
Jingle bells, jingle bells
Jingle all the way
Oh, what fun it is to ride
In a one horse open sleigh

A day or two ago
I thought I'd take a ride

And soon Miss Fanny Bright
Was seated by my side
The horse was lean and lank
Misfortune seemed his lot
We got into a drifted bank
And then we got upsot

Oh, jingle bells, jingle bells
Jingle all the way
Oh, what fun it is to ride
In a one horse open sleigh
Jingle bells, jingle bells
Jingle all the way
Oh, what fun it is to ride
In a one horse open sleigh yeah

Jingle bells, jingle bells
Jingle all the way
Oh, what fun it is to ride
In a one horse open sleigh
Jingle bells, jingle bells
Jingle all the way
Oh, what fun it is to ride
In a one horse open sleigh

2. We Wish you a Merry Christmas

We wish you a Merry Christmas;
We wish you a Merry Christmas;
We wish you a Merry Christmas and a Happy New Year.
Good tidings we bring to you and your kin;
Good tidings for Christmas and a Happy New Year.

Oh, bring us a figgy pudding;
Oh, bring us a figgy pudding;
Oh, bring us a figgy pudding and a cup of good cheer
We won't go until we get some;
We won't go until we get some;
We won't go until we get some, so bring some out here

We wish you a Merry Christmas;
We wish you a Merry Christmas;
We wish you a Merry Christmas and a Happy New Year.

3. Rudolph the Red-Nosed Reindeer

Rudolph, the red-nosed reindeer
had a very shiny nose.
And if you ever saw him,
you would even say it glows.

All of the other reindeer
used to laugh and call him names.
They never let poor Rudolph
join in any reindeer games.

Then one foggy Christmas Eve
Santa came to say:
'Rudolph with your nose so bright,
won't you guide my sleigh tonight?'

Then all the reindeer loved him
as they shouted out with glee,
Rudolph the red-nosed reindeer,
you'll go down in history!

4. Silent Night

Silent night, holy night
All is calm, all is bright
Round yon Virgin Mother and Child
Holy Infant so tender and mild
Sleep in heavenly peace
Sleep in heavenly peace

Silent night, holy night!
Shepherds quake at the sight
Glories stream from heaven afar
Heavenly hosts sing Alleluia!
Christ, the Saviour is born
Christ, the Saviour is born

Silent night, holy night
Son of God, love's pure light
Radiant beams from Thy holy face
With the dawn of redeeming grace
Jesus, Lord, at Thy birth
Jesus, Lord, at Thy birth

5. Santa Claus is Coming to Town

You better watch out
You better not cry
Better not pout
I'm telling you why
Santa Claus is coming to town
He's making a list
And checking it twice;
Gonna find out Who's naughty and nice
Santa Claus is coming to town

He sees you when you're sleeping
He knows when you're awake
He knows if you've been bad or good
So be good for goodness sake!
O! You better watch out!
You better not cry
Better not pout
I'm telling you why
Santa Claus is coming to town
Santa Claus is coming to town

6. Deck the Halls

Deck the halls with boughs of holly,
Fa la la la la, la la la la.
Tis the season to be jolly,
Fa la la la la, la la la la.

Don we now our gay apparel,
Fa la la, la la la, la la la.
Troll the ancient Yule tide carol,
Fa la la la la, la la la la.

See the blazing Yule before us,
Fa la la la la, la la la la.

Strike the harp and join the chorus.
Fa la la la la, la la la la.

Follow me in merry measure,
Fa la la la la, la la la la.
While I tell of Yule tide treasure,
Fa la la la la, la la la la.

Fast away the old year passes,
Fa la la la la, la la la la.
Hail the new, ye lads and lasses,
Fa la la la la, la la la la.

Festivals Rock!
Diary

Keep all your memories of Christmas right here, in our special diary!

Everyone I met this Christmas:

Everyone I celebrated Christmas with:

Everywhere I went this Christmas:

Everything I ate this Christmas:

All the gifts I gave this Christmas:

All the gifts I got, in return:

What I want to do next Christmas:

The most fun memory I have this Christmas:

Draw your favourite moments from this year's festivities on the next two pages, or if you have photographs, paste them here:

Notes on the Contributors

Anu Kumar has held and given up several jobs but remained faithful to her first love, writing. Her books for children and young adults include the MythQuest series (Hachette India), *Atisa and the Seven Wonders* and *In the Country of Gold Digging Ants*, both published by Penguin/Puffin. She was awarded for her stories by the Commonwealth Broadcasting Association in 2004, and *The Little Magazine* in 2006. She has also written two novels for adults.

Rituparna Chatterjee lives a sci-fi life, thanks to her day job as a science and technology journalist in Silicon Valley. For play she transforms her discoveries into children's fiction and dreamy desserts. But that is only when she is not being followed by stray robot puppies obsessed with adopting her! Better known as the Purple Fairy of the Lost Woods, she arms children in the San Francisco Bay Area with floral chocolate wands and takes them on all kinds of adventures. Join the Purple Fairy on her adventures on www.readrituparna.com or on Twitter @ReadRituparna.

Deepa Agarwal has written more than 40 books for children and adults. *Caravan to Tibet* (Penguin/Puffin, 2007), selected for the Ibby Honour List 2008 as the best book from India, and a translation of the famous Hindi classic *Chandrakanta* (Penguin/Puffin, 2008) are two of her recent titles. Deepa has won the NCERT National Award for her picture book, *Ashok's New Friends* (Children's Book Trust). Five of her books have been listed in the White Raven Catalogue brought out by the IYL, Munich.

Sangeeta Basu is the co-founder of iThink Learning, an organization engaged in consultancy in education. Her work is with learners of all age groups and across schools, NGOs, professional institutes and corporate houses. iThink conducts workshops across India to encourage learners to understand themselves as their own richest resource by identifying and activating their own potential. Sangeeta writes stories and poems for children.

Swapna Dutta has been writing, mostly for children, for the last four decades and has more than 40 titles to her credit, including translations. She has been published by HarperCollins, Scholastic, Orient Longman, Rupa, Children's Book Trust and National Book Trust, among others, and has also worked as Editorial Consultant for *Target* (Living Media), Assistant Editor for *Limca Book of Records* and Deputy Editor for Encyclopaedia Britannica between 1988 and 2002.

Ani Sengupta believes he is an animator who creates new characters and plays them in various settings. His young friends give him ideas for characters and incidents that he adds to his animation and together they make new stories. When Ani is not animating, he likes to visit scary places and play extreme sports like sky diving.

Roopa Pai is the author of Taranauts (www.taranauts.com), India's first fantasy-adventure series for children. She contributes regularly to children's magazines *Hoot* and *Toot*, and writes a weekly history column for the student edition of *Deccan Herald*. She also leads history and heritage tours for children as part of Bangalore Walks. She can be reached at roopa.pai@gmail.com.

Subhamoy Das is a former journalist and communications professional currently based in Hyderabad. He started writing for children's magazines as a teenager, contributes regularly for *Target*, *Teens Today*, *PCM Magazine* and *Children's Digest*. He has worked for several years as a journalist, illustrator and multimedia editor with India's leading media companies. Since 1999, Subhamoy has been writing extensively on Hindu philosophy and Indian culture, for his popular blog hinduism.about.com, a top-tier website owned by the New York Times Company.

Urvashi Bahuguna grew up in Goa, and is now pursuing a degree in English Literature at St. Stephen's College, Delhi. She contributes regularly to *Helter Skelter*, an indie journal on alternative culture in India. She writes as an excuse to avoid doing other things and is in the middle of organizing her doodles into her first book. Some of her babble can be found at www.howkhemiabecamealchemy.blogspot.com.

9789350093429